Assessing APEC's Progress

The **Institute of Southeast Asian Studies (ISEAS)** was established as an autonomous organization in 1968. It is a regional research centre for scholars and other specialists concerned with modern Southeast Asia, particularly the many-faceted problems of stability and security, economic development, and political and social change.

The Institute's research programmes are the Regional Economic Studies (RES, including ASEAN and APEC), Regional Strategic and Political Studies (RSPS), and Regional Social and Cultural Studies (RSCS).

The Institute is governed by a twenty-two-member Board of Trustees comprising nominees from the Singapore Government, the National University of Singapore, the various Chambers of Commerce, and professional and civic organizations. A ten-man Executive Committee oversees day-to-day operations; it is chaired by the Director, the Institute's chief academic and administrative officer.

A Project of the APEC International Assessment Network (APIAN)

Assessing APEC's Progress
Trade, Ecotech & Institutions

Edited by
Richard E. Feinberg and **Ye Zhao**

Institute of Southeast Asian Studies
Singapore

Published by
Institute of Southeast Asian Studies
30 Heng Mui Keng Terrace
Pasir Panjang
Singapore 119614
Internet e-mail: publish@iseas.edu.sg
World Wide Web: http://www.iseas.edu.sg/pub.html

The responsibility for facts and opinions expressed in this publication rests exclusively with the editors and authors and their interpretations do not necessarily reflect the views or the policy of the Institute.

ISEAS Library Cataloguing-in-Publication Data

Assessing APEC's progress: trade, ecotech, and institutions / edited by Richard Feinberg and Ye Zhao.
1. Asian Pacific Economic Cooperation.
2. Asia—Commercial policy.
3. Pacific Area—Commercial policy.
4. Asia—Economic policy.
5. Pacific Area—Economic policy.
6. Technological innovations—Asia.
7. Technological innovations—Pacific Area.
8. Finance—Asia.
9. Finance—Pacific Area.
I. Feinberg, Richard E.
II. Ye, Zhao.

HF1583 A84 2001 sls2001014795

ISBN 981-230-143-7

Typeset by Scientifik Graphics (Singapore) Pte Ltd
Printed in Singapore by Seng Lee Press Pte Ltd.

CONTENTS

THE CONTRIBUTORS

Richard E. Feinberg (Project Co-ordinator) is Director of the APEC Study Centre, Graduate School of International Relations and Pacific Studies (IR/PS), University of California, San Diego, USA.

Ye Zhao is Research Associate in the APEC Study Centre, Graduate School of International Relations and Pacific Studies (IR/PS), University of California, San Diego, USA.

Chen-Sheng Ho is at the APEC Study Centre, Taiwan Institute of Economic Research, Chinese Taipei.

Myrna S. Austria is Director of the Philippine APEC Study Centre Network and Secretariat of the Philippine Institute for Development Studies, Philippines.

Merit E. Janow is Co-Director of the APEC Study Centre, Columbia University, USA.

Leonardo A. Lanzona is Chair of the Economics Department, Ateneo de Manila University, Philippines.

Jianren Lu is Deputy Director of the Institute of Asia-Pacific Studies, Chinese Academy of Social Sciences, China.

Glen Taylor is Deputy Director of the APEC Study Centre, College of Business Administration, University of Hawaii at Manoa, USA.

Robert Scollay is Director of the APEC Study Centre, University of Auckland, New Zealand.

Neantro Saavedra-Rivano is Director of the APEC Study Centre, Graduate School of International Political Economy, University of Tsukuba, Japan.

John McKay is Director of the Australian APEC Study Centre and Monash Asia Institute, Monash University, Australia.

Michael G. Plummer is Associate Professor of the Graduate School of International Economics, Brandeis University, USA.

Vinod K. Aggarwal is Director of the Berkeley APEC Study Centre, University of California, Berkeley, USA.

Kun-Chin Lin is Project Director of the Berkeley APEC Study Centre, University of California, Berkeley, USA.

INTRODUCTION

This book is the result of two years of planning and research that began in January 1999, when a group of scholars held a brainstorming session in La Jolla, California. We all had a strong interest in APEC (Asia-Pacific Economic Cooperation) and were seeking ways to increase the linkages between the scholarly and non-governmental communities and APEC officials. We felt strongly that APEC could benefit from such expert interaction, from the knowledge and experience scholars and outside experts can bring to the table, from their independent, critical perspectives, and from their channels of influence with broader public opinion.

APEC has from time to time expressed its interest in working more closely with outside experts, and in 1993 APEC established APEC Study Centres (ASCs) to promote research, dissemination and regional cooperation. In the intervening years, some APEC Working Groups have drawn on external expertise. But often APEC has kept non-governmental experts at arms length, perhaps fearing that such interactions might be shallow or contentious. Some APEC members expressed concerns that interactions with outside groups might favour some APEC economies over others. Questions have also been raised about the representativeness of possible interlocutors.

At the La Jolla meeting, we came up with a formula that we believe provides APEC with the benefits of expert input while avoiding the potential pitfalls. We have involved leading experts with years of experience in their areas of research, and in studying the economic and political trends in the Asia-Pacific. Many have dedicated themselves to advancing the causes of regional integration and cooperation, and hence share the fundamental purposes and aspirations of APEC. There would be no reason, therefore, for tedious or contentious exchanges. We dealt with the issue of potential asymmetries by forming a balanced, comprehensive group with members from throughout the Asia-Pacific: industrial and developing countries, North and South, Asia and the Western Hemisphere. And we solved the potential problem of representation by basing our activities on ASCs which enjoy the official imprimatur of the APEC leaders.

At the La Jolla meeting, representatives from ASCs located in nine APEC member economies decided to launch the experiment we call the APEC International Assessment Network — APIAN, for short. APIAN's mission statement is straightforward: to track and assess the design and execution of select APEC initiatives, to enhance knowledge among government officials and the general public with regard to APEC activities, to encourage the fulfilment of APEC objectives and commitments, and to identify ways for APEC to improve its performance.

Since the seminal La Jolla conclave, many other ASCs have joined in APIAN activities. APIAN has met on the margins of the annual ASC international consortium meetings, and in October 2000, the Institute of Southeast Asian Studies (ISEAS) in Singapore hosted an important APIAN workshop.

Section 1 of this volume includes APIAN's first major Policy Report, *Learning From Experience*. Its 22 signatories are leading scholars at ASCs from 13 APEC member economies: Australia, Canada, Chile, China, Hong Kong, Japan, New Zealand, Philippines, Singapore, South Korea, Chinese Taipei, Thailand, and the United States.

With the generous assistance of the APEC Secretariat, *Learning From Experience* received wide distribution at the Leaders' Meeting in Brunei in November 2000. Press attention included opinion editorials written by APIAN members. In response to the Policy Report, the February 2001 Senior Officials Meeting (SOM) formally took note of APIAN, and the Ecotech Sub-committee of SOM officially invited a representative of APIAN to its next meeting to discuss *Learning From Experience* and to suggest how to proceed on the future evaluation of Ecotech activities. *Learning From Experience* is posted on the official APEC Secretariat website, and APIAN is listed on the website's glossary of key abbreviations. The first APIAN Policy Report has also been posted on many ASC websites, and has been translated into Chinese.

Learning From Experience assesses APEC's successes and failures and advances 12 major policy recommendations to improve APEC's performance, with regard to Trade and Investment Liberalization and Facilitation (TILF), Economic and Technical Cooperation (Ecotech), and Institutional Structures. The recommendations — which are summarized in the Policy Report's Executive Summary — are specific and action-oriented and APIAN intends to track APEC's reactions and to continue to press for their full implementation.

Learning From Experience was informed by a series of Issue Reports on specific APEC activities. These Issue Reports are made public in revised and updated form for the first time in Section II of this volume. Issues covered include services, investment policy, competition and regulatory reform, mobility of business people, human resource development, food and agriculture, industrial science and technology, energy, economic infrastructure, corporate governance, financial stability, and APEC as an institution. Prepared by APIAN participants, these Issue Reports generally follow a common format: a summary of the key initiatives in the issue area that have been approved by APEC; actions taken at the international level; actions taken at the level of member economies; evaluation of progress; assessment of strengths and weaknesses; and recommendations. To augment existing information sources, the authors of the Issue Reports designed and circulated questionnaires to other experts in APEC member economies; for illustrative purposes, one such questionnaire is included as an appendix to the Issue Report on financial stability.

This volume contains the products of APIAN's first phase. We will continue to monitor and evaluate APEC's performance, with the ultimate objective of enhancing mutual prosperity and cooperation in the Asia-Pacific. In addition to issuing periodic policy reports, we will look for new ways to interact with official APEC to encourage the fulfilment of APEC objectives and commitments. In these activities, we welcome the participation of other scholars and non-governmental experts that share APIAN's purposes, just as we look forward to productive interactions with APEC officials.

APIAN's progress and this volume would not have been possible without the sincere collaboration of many institutions and individuals. The APIAN project has enjoyed the generous support of the Institute on Global Conflict and Cooperation (IGCC) of the University of California and the Japan Foundation Centre for Global Partnership (CGP). The preparation of this book benefited from the support and encouragement of the ISEAS Director, Professor Chia Siow Yue, and the Institute's superb editorial staff. My co-editor, Ye Zhao, was an outstanding project manager and a joy to have as a colleague. Xin Wang, Research Assistant at the APEC Study Centre, University of California at San Diego, was responsible for the Chinese translation of *Learning From Experience*.

Richard Feinberg
La Jolla, California
March 2001

SECTION I

POLICY REPORT

3 - 36

NA
no autha

1

LEARNING FROM EXPERIENCE
The First APIAN Policy Report

EXECUTIVE SUMMARY

The APEC International Assessment Network (APIAN) is a collaborative, independent project among participating APEC Study Centres to track and assess the design and execution of select Asia-Pacific Economic Cooperation (APEC) initiatives. APIAN's mission is to enhance knowledge among government officials and the general public with regard to APEC activities, to encourage the fulfilment of APEC objectives and commitments, and to identify ways for APEC to improve its performance.

We believe that APEC has many accomplishments to its credit. APEC has established itself as a world-class forum where leaders, bureaucrats, and private sector executives meet regularly in diverse settings to exchange ideas and to advance common goals. We believe that the annual Leaders' Meetings are especially valuable; while a degree of scripted orchestration is to be expected, we recommend that Leaders' Meetings allow ample opportunity for free-flowing communication and real decision-making, letting leaders be leaders.

APEC has contributed to the affirmation and dissemination of a coherent set of positive ideas. It has promoted a liberal international order, and its "open regionalism" asserts that regional integration is consistent with globalism. APEC working groups and task forces promote the sharing of "best practices" among members. It is catalyzing the gathering of information and construction of databases on a wide range of issues. APEC was among the first international institutions to closely link economic and technical cooperation to trade and investment liberalization.

As APEC enters its second decade, it faces a tough list of challenges. If it fails to respond, many people may come to perceive APEC as comprising ritualistic diplomatic meetings that have little relevance to their daily lives. When leaders do respond to new opportunities with bold initiatives, APEC will lose credibility unless effective implementation follows.

Trade and Investment Liberalization and Facilitation (TILF)

We attribute the apparent lack of value-added of APEC's TILF to several factors, including the slow adaptation of the APEC agenda, the absence of priorities, shortfalls in members' commitments, weak evaluation procedures, and the dearth of specific APEC incentives. To enhance APEC's performance on TILF, we recommend:

1. *APEC should clarify and prioritize some of its trade policy initiatives.* In some complex issue areas, such as services and competition policy, APEC should consider prioritizing select sub-sectors or actionable items. We also recommend that APEC establish priority areas for immediate progress in trade and investment liberalization, such as national treatment, non-tariff barriers and tariff peaks, and export subsidies.
2. *APEC should continue to improve its individual action plans (IAPs).* IAP commitments should be specific, concrete and measurable to the extent possible.
3. *APEC members should be accountable for their IAP commitments.* We call upon APEC to establish effective mechanisms — both internal and external to APEC — for the review of members' IAP commitments and implementation. The IAP peer reviews should call for more rigorous commentaries. APEC should continue to call upon outside, independent experts to evaluate its TILF programmes.

Economic and Technical Cooperation (Ecotech)

Ecotech is critical to the realization of APEC's vision and the economic development of APEC members. Yet, Ecotech suffers from a number of shortcomings, including the excessive diffusion of limited Ecotech resources, the proliferation of Ecotech forums, the lack of coordination around defined APEC objectives, inadequate authority allowed to the Ecotech Subcommittee, and too little funding for Ecotech initiatives.

To enable APEC to overcome the current crisis of confidence in its Ecotech programmes, we recommend:

1. *APEC should overhaul its Ecotech programmes.* APEC needs to streamline Ecotech programmes, to set priorities, to rationalize working groups, and to improve coordination among Ecotech forums. The Ecotech Subcommittee should be given more authority and resources to pursue its mandates.
2. *Ecotech needs more active funding.* APEC should encourage the resource-rich multilateral development banks to fund sound Ecotech projects. More organic ties should also be pursued with bilateral donors. Private-sector involvement in specific projects should also be systematically encouraged. We suggest that consideration be given to establishing "Ecotech Funds" that would use APEC creativity to catalyze financial support from these public and private sources behind APEC priorities.
3. *APEC should mandate action plans for Ecotech.* Individual and collective action plans should be prepared for Ecotech. To assure coherence and succinctness, such action plans should be restricted to APEC-specific programmes and projects. In their IAPs, members should specify both commitments and implementation results, and include timetables and quantifiable targets to the extent possible.

Institutional Structures

APEC will fall well short of its goals if it does not find a better match between its aspirations and its institutional structures. Therefore, we recommend:

1. *The APEC Secretariat should be strengthened.* A stronger Secretariat that has more in-house capacity to monitor the implementation of APEC initiatives can help APEC to better evaluate, rationalize, and coordinate both TILF and Ecotech. To strengthen the Secretariat, we propose the creation of longer-term professional positions and the designation of a Secretary-General with a multi-year term of office.
2. *APEC should deepen its ties with other international and regional organizations.* We urge Ecotech to seek support from multilateral development banks that share APEC objectives. TILF forums should deepen their relations with the World Trade Organization (WTO) and other relevant multilateral forums. APEC should consult more routinely with other regional trade arrangements, such that their gains in liberalization are constructively nested under APEC.

3. *Ministries of Finance should be better integrated into the APEC process.* The post-financial crisis agenda demands that APEC better integrate finance and development.
4. *Partnerships with outside groups should be strengthened.* APIAN questionnaires suggest that strong business and civil society participation contributes to the successful implementation of APEC initiatives. Business should be involved in all stages of the project cycle. We believe that NGO involvement with select working groups, such as those responsible for the environment, human resource development, gender equality, and micro-enterprises, would be particularly beneficial.
5. *Academic engagement should be encouraged.* To help build a broadly based Pacific community of intellectuals, APEC should reach out more systematically to universities and policy institutes. APIAN — as a voluntary grouping of APEC Study Centres — is convinced that APEC can take better advantage of the Centres' capacities and goodwill.
6. *APEC should augment its dissemination efforts.* APIAN questionnaires revealed a stunning lack of public awareness of APEC activities. A better-staffed Secretariat should devote more resources to dissemination and outreach to non-governmental groups. Broader and more systematic engagement with the private sector and other non-governmental groups would be an important component of an energized effort to broaden APEC's base. It is only through deep and broad dialogue that APEC can realize its core mission — to foster a community of nations and peoples in the Asia-Pacific.

APIAN'S MISSION

The APEC International Assessment Network is a collaborative, independent project among participating APEC Study Centres to track and assess the design and execution of select APEC initiatives. APIAN's mission is to enhance know-ledge among government officials and the general public with regard to APEC activities, to encourage the fulfilment of APEC objectives and commitments, and to identify ways for APEC to improve its performance.

Since 1989, and especially since APEC leaders began holding annual summits in 1993, APEC forums have been generating a series of official declarations replete with hundreds of action items. These initiatives cover critically important matters, including trade integration, financial stability, environmental protection, human resource development, and other areas of economic and technical cooperation. The strategic intention is that multilateral cooperation on these vital development issues will help to build a prosperous and peaceful Pacific community of nations.

Important as these objectives are, there has been no ongoing, comprehensive, and independent effort to track and evaluate the implementation of APEC initiatives and to determine whether there has been progress from "words to deeds". With the lack of such efforts, external evaluations have several deleterious effects. Without effective information, the scholarly community and civil society in general are largely ignorant of, and sceptical towards APEC. Without transparency and public debate, APEC officials may not feel obliged to act upon official promises. With little scholarly input, APEC is deprived of valuable sources of expert information and critical feedback.

To meet this need for independent evaluation, representatives from APEC Study Centres located in nine APEC member economies convened in January 1999 at the University of California, San Diego, to launch the APIAN experiment, and invited other centres to participate on a voluntary basis. Since then, many other centres have joined in APIAN activities. Subsequent APIAN meetings were held during the annual international consortium meeting of APEC Study Centres in Auckland in June 1999, and in Brunei in May 2000. On 6–7 October 2000, the Institute of Southeast Asian Studies (ISEAS) hosted a workshop in Singapore to finalize this Report. The APIAN project has also benefited from the encouragement and support of the Institute on Global Conflict and Cooperation (IGCC) of the University of California.

APIAN participants served as Issue Coordinators who prepared Issue Reports on specific APEC initiatives. These Issue Reports were used as background papers for this Report. In preparing their reports, Issue Coordinators relied on several sources of information. They designed and circulated questionnaires to experts in APEC member economies. The APEC Study Centre at the Taiwan Institute of Economic Research (TIER) was responsible for the circulation of issue questionnaires. These questionnaires yielded valuable indicative information; however, due to time and other constraints, the response rate was uneven and the number of responses was too small to qualify as a scientific sample. Issue Coordinators also drew on the research of other scholars, and on the valuable publications of such informed organizations as the Pacific Economic Cooperation Council (PECC), the Pacific Trade and Development Conference (PAFTAD), and the APEC Business Advisory Council (ABAC). The APEC Secretariat in Singapore was generous in its assistance and responded to issue questionnaires. As experts in their chosen fields, APIAN Issue Coordinators could also draw on their own accumulated expertise, and in numerous cases, their previous work with APEC. A list of Issue Coordinators can be found in the appendix.

This Report does not attempt to assess all of APEC's work. Rather, we have selected areas of APEC activity that we believe to be particularly important and where we have expertise. We are confident, however, that APIAN gathered sufficient information and experience to render general judgements on APEC performance, as well as to offer specific recommendations.

We have discussed APIAN's objectives with many government officials involved in APEC activities, and we have been very gratified with their enthusiasm for our purposes. We look forward to discussing our assessments and recommendations with them.

This report is a collaborative effort by a large number of APEC Study Centres from many APEC member economies. The participating experts wholeheartedly endorse this report's overall content and tone and support its principal findings and recommendations, even as each participant may not agree fully with every phrase. The participating experts subscribe as individuals; institutional affiliations are for purposes of identification only. The list of signatories can be found in Appendix A. APIAN does not purport to speak for all APEC Study Centres, nor for the international consortium of APEC Study Centres.

UNDERSTANDING APEC

We aspire to be realists and idealists at the same time. We must recognize the constraints that bind the aspirations of APEC member populations and that limit the margin for manoeuvre of governments. In the past, the great diversity and heterogeneity that divided the Asia-Pacific left the region bereft of cooperative inter-governmental institutions. These deeply rooted divisions can only be relaxed slowly. But we also believe that visionary ideas and bold political leadership can overcome history and create a more peaceful and prosperous future. We believe that the peoples of the Asia-Pacific are increasingly reaching out to each other and are ready for more cooperative ventures.

APEC itself is a unique blend of realism and idealism. The very idea of an association of nations and economies that span the vast Pacific Ocean — that seeks to transform the world's largest body of water from a deep divide into a bridge among peoples — and that seeks to build cooperative relations among former rival states, is profoundly visionary. And APEC's early leaders have built on these visionary foundations with bold initiatives. The promise of free trade and investment flows throughout the Asia-Pacific is breathtaking in its implications, not only for future economic relations but also for the political cooperation that almost certainly must follow.

In its pursuit of these ambitions, APEC has been realistic in its choice of modalities. APEC's core principles — consensus, voluntarism and unilateralism — derive precisely from a sagacious recognition of the steep barriers to economic openness and to regional cooperation erected during past centuries. APEC members will either move forward at their own pace, in response to their own domestic interests and capacities, or they will not move forward together at all. APEC members can try to persuade and cajole, and even embarrass fellow members into collective action, but they will not accept impositions and rules imposed by even a majority. APEC members will consider guidelines, but they will reject bindings. Furthermore, APEC recognizes that global integration poses formidable challenges and that governments must actively build strong domestic market-oriented institutions and help to educate a competitive workforce; APEC's Ecotech initiatives are responsive to this contemporary reality.

APEC's particular blend of idealism and realism has produced a "soft" or "weak" institution, as the APIAN Issue Report on APEC as an Institution explains. Unlike such established agencies as the International Monetary Fund (IMF) and the World Bank, APEC has no executive board with decision-making authority. Unlike the WTO, APEC can neither "bind" trade agreements nor authorize punitive actions against members whose trade policies are inconsistent with APEC norms. Unlike the Organization for European Cooperation and Development (OECD), APEC has no expert bureaucracy capable at times of driving policy through its own initiative. Unlike the Association for Southeast Asian Nations (ASEAN), APEC's Secretariat lacks the internal capacity to monitor and evaluate the implementation of key APEC programmes. All of this is by conscious design: in their realism, APEC members refused to grant such powers to their fledgling association. They were not prepared to allocate such authority to a collective agency.

However "soft", APEC has evolved into an institution. Brick by brick, APEC has been constructing its edifice. During its first decade, APEC has created a set of norms, procedures and structures that define its essence: the goal of free trade and investment flows within a paradigm of open regionalism; capacity-building through economic and technical cooperation; agreement through consensus action by each member at its own pace; annual Leaders' Meetings and regularly scheduled Ministerial Meetings that set direction; committees of senior officials that drive the process; and an array of working groups responsible for specific programmes and projects. APEC has established its special place in the panoply of international institutions.

We believe that this soft institutionalism served APEC well during its infancy. Many of those who criticize APEC for not accomplishing more fail to understand the nature of "soft" institutionalism and why the region's realities allowed no other choice. We also believe that as APEC enters its second decade, it must constantly engage in serious self-examination. It must consider whether its "soft" institutionalism is facilitating decision-making, whether the vision and mandates of its leaders are being transformed into tangible actions, and whether APEC officials are receiving the critical feedback integral to sound governance.

What may have been realistic at the outset may have become an avoidable obstacle to further achievement. What may have seemed hopelessly idealist at the beginning may have become more feasible as members gain confidence in APEC and in each other. What seemed dangerous may now appear comfortable and even desirable.

APEC'S ACHIEVEMENTS AND CHALLENGES

We believe that APEC has many accomplishments to its credit. We reach this conclusion based upon APIAN-generated research, other studies and reports, including those published by APEC, and our own accumulated experience.

APEC as a World-Class Forum

APEC has established itself as a world-class forum where leaders, bureaucrats, and private-sector executives meet regularly in diverse settings to exchange ideas and to advance common goals. In a region as vast and diverse as the Asia-Pacific, this is no mean feat. Before the advent of modern means of travel and communication, an institution as meeting-intensive as APEC could not have flourished. APEC is as much a product of globalization as it is a response to its challenges.

We believe that the annual Leaders' Meetings are especially valuable, an opinion confirmed by respondents to our questionnaires. These summits provide a unique opportunity for the region's leaders to meet in both plurilateral and bilateral settings and to exchange views on the APEC agenda as well as on a wide range of issues of mutual interest. The informal venues allow for the development of personal "chemistry" and friendships that facilitate future decision-making. APEC's regularly scheduled gatherings are particularly opportune during moments of diplomatic stress. The annual summits are also valuable in giving leaders a regular opportunity to reaffirm the APEC vision, to establish broad policy guidelines, and to review the APEC workplan.

Leaders' Meetings have two other important procedural advantages. When a Leaders' Meeting is on the calendar, bureaucrats know that they may be held accountable for their implementation of previously-mandated initiatives. As the Leaders' Meeting approaches, governments focus their attention on APEC and more generally, on the Asia-Pacific region. The Leaders' Meetings set deadlines for decisions — within member governments as well as among APEC members. The Meetings themselves provide the opportunity for leaders to break bureaucratic logjams and resolve difficult issues among themselves. Notably, it is doubtful that the Bogor goals of free and open trade in the region would have been approved without the impetus of summitry. Respondents to APIAN's questionnaire regarding APEC as an institution gave high marks to the Leaders' Meetings as the most effective negotiating forum for APEC. While a degree of scripted orchestration is to be expected, we recommend that Leaders' Meetings allow ample opportunity for free-flowing communication and real decision-making, letting leaders be leaders.

Leaders' Meetings also allow for statesmen to interact with representatives from the private sector, as the exchanges with ABAC and the CEO Forum attest. In a few cases, Leaders' Meetings have also allowed for interactions with other civil society groups.

Certainly, the annual summits gather thousands of journalists, offering APEC leaders a wonderful opportunity to explain APEC's purposes to the broader public.

We also believe that the myriad of other APEC meetings — the ministerials, committees and working groups — are essential to APEC's progress. However, as we spell out below, the organizational structure that has grown piecemeal over time is now in need of serious revision.

APEC as a Driver of Ideas

We believe that ideas matter in history. One reason for the collapse of the WTO ministerial meeting in Seattle in 1999 was the widespread fear that globalization is a threat to the well-being of the majority of peoples. We fully recognize that globalization causes serious social disruptions that must be addressed, and we believe that some assessments of globalization mis-identify the causes of some of the world's problems, while some critics of globalization advocate ideas that could endanger the future prosperity and security of the Asia-Pacific.

APEC has contributed to the affirmation and dissemination of a coherent set of positive ideas. In its adherence to the Bogor vision of free and open commerce in the Asia-Pacific, APEC has promoted a liberal internationalist order. As a flag carrier for economic reform and trade liberalization, APEC adds its voice to those forces within member economies that advocate similar goals. During the 1997–98 financial crisis, the APEC vision reinforced those who sought to adjust their economies by advancing market-oriented reforms, not by reverting to national measures destructive to regional prosperity. Indeed, in the wake of the crisis, many APEC governments have further opened their economies, notably with regard to their treatment of direct investment.

APEC's "open regionalism" asserts that regional integration is consistent with globalism. Liberalization in the Asia-Pacific must be a building block towards global free trade and investment flows — not a threat to divide the world into rival trading blocs. APEC has not defined "open regionalism" with precision, but its members clearly seek compatibility between APEC's economic initiatives and the goals and principles of the WTO. In response to the resurgent interest in regional and sub-regional free trade arrangements, we believe that APEC has a role to play in reviewing such arrangements for consistency with APEC and WTO purposes.

APEC working groups and task forces promote the sharing of "best practices" among members. There are many examples where members have benefited from the experiences of other economies. APEC has facilitated conferences and training sessions on such important topics as corporate governance, financial supervision, competition policy, electronic commerce, educational reform, and efficient energy production, among many others. Such events may over time yield a gradual "soft" convergence of ideas and practices.

APEC is catalyzing the gathering of information and construction of databases on a wide range of issues. As pedestrian as they may seem, databases can make important contributions to transparency, monitoring, evaluation, and the sharing of best practices. For example, the APIAN Issue Report on Industrial Science and Technology found that perhaps the most useful action taken by APEC in that area has been the creation of the APEC Science and Technology Web (AST Web). APEC's databases are often imperfect, as officials struggle to standardize data across many economies, to clarify terms and categories, to elicit more precise and timely information, and to design user-friendly formats. Yet improvement is evident, for example, in the IAPs which document members' commitments towards attaining the Bogor goals.

APEC was among the first international institutions to closely link economic and technical cooperation to trade and investment liberalization. APEC understands that for developing countries to achieve the Bogor goals, they must prepare their economic structures and workforces to benefit from globalization. The promotion of human resource development, the diffusion of information technology, and the strengthening of social safety nets are critical to successful market-oriented economic development. As APIAN researchers and many others have commented, Ecotech has so far fallen short of its promise, but APEC is on the right track.

In a region better known for its historic rivalries than for intergovernmental cooperation, APEC has sought to foster the notion of a Pacific community that encompasses East Asia as well as much of the Western Hemisphere. APEC has helped to fashion an *esprit de corps* among the officials participating in the various APEC forums, and has taken some steps to catalyze increased activities among the region's private sector and academic institutions. It remains to be seen, however, whether this expansive vision will take root and flourish.

Challenges

As APEC enters its second decade, it faces a tough list of challenges. The global development community continues to differ on the efficacy and equity of various models of economic development, and the Asia-Pacific community is at the vortex of this contentious debate. While it was unfair to blame APEC for the 1997-98 financial crisis, as APEC had not been set up to tackle finance, populations do expect APEC to play a larger role in sustaining the recovery. Similarly, the recent hike in oil prices lies outside APEC's jurisdiction, and APEC members are not necessarily in agreement on short-term remedies, but the APEC energy forums can offer longer-term answers. In the trade area, where APEC has concentrated much of its efforts, the collapse of the Seattle Ministerial Meeting raises questions about APEC's reliance on a prospective WTO round as the main avenue for maintaining momentum towards the Bogor goals. If APEC fails to respond adequately to such urgent matters, sceptics may come to perceive APEC as consisting of ritualistic diplomatic meetings that have little relevance to their daily lives.

Regional trends pose additional challenges. The sudden surge of proposals for new bilateral and plurilateral subregional trading arrangements raises anew old questions about whether these preferential deals may be building blocks or stumbling blocks towards the achievement of region-wide free trade, and how APEC should react to these new initiatives in ways which encourage their compatibility with APEC and WTO goals. Furthermore, new forms of political cooperation among Asian nations have emerged, such as the ASEAN plus Three (Japan, China, South Korea) initiative. To some degree, such regional initiatives may reflect frustration with APEC. Such initiatives could drain energy away from APEC, or alternatively, could spur APEC to more decisive action.

When APEC leaders do respond to new challenges and opportunities with bold, far-reaching initiatives, APEC will lose credibility unless effective implementation follows. When launching important initiatives, APEC must ensure that an appropriate framework is put in place for effective implementation, and for holding officials accountable for that implementation. We note that too often, APEC policy-makers have paid inadequate attention to implementation; for example, the APIAN Issue Report on Food and Agriculture raised serious concerns regarding the credibility of APEC's implementation of the APEC Food System proposals.

APEC must overcome a public perception of ineffectiveness. To regain its momentum, APEC needs some visible successes — and to make them known to the broader public. APEC must also get its own house in order. It needs to clarify its agenda, set priorities and revamp its internal structures. In the following section, we examine some of these critical challenges and propose pathways to greater Asia-Pacific economic cooperation.

RECOMMENDATIONS FOR IMPROVING APEC'S PERFORMANCE

It is only natural that a young institution with the ambition and complexity of APEC would experience growing pains. Among the comments on APEC's performance, there is widespread consensus on many of the institution's shortcomings. Some of these shortcomings are common to multilateral endeavours and will be very hard to overcome. Other weaknesses are concessions to realism that can be addressed only gradually. However, as we propose below, some of these flaws can and must be confronted today if APEC is to move forward.

We group our assessments of APEC's performance under three broad headings: trade and investment liberalization and facilitation, economic and technical cooperation, and APEC as an institution. We conclude each section with our recommendations for enhancing APEC's performance.

Trade and Investment Liberalization and Facilitation (TILF)

TILF has been at the heart of APEC's efforts throughout its first decade. Yet, APIAN's research reaffirms the conclusions of numerous other studies that it is difficult to attribute significant liberalization in most APEC members to APEC *per se*. We attribute TILF's apparent lack of value-added to several factors, and we are convinced that corrective measures are feasible:

- *Slow adaptation of the APEC agenda.* In some areas, the APEC agenda is lagging behind circumstances, or APEC's own experience. For example, in the increasingly important areas of competition policy and non-tariff barriers (NTBs), the 1995 Osaka Action Agenda would benefit from being updated: APEC's NTB agenda is insufficiently specific and omits important items. Furthermore, it is now time to make provision for member economies to specify how they will apply the APEC Principles on Competition and Regulatory Reform in particular situations. The proliferation of negotiations on sub-regional trading arrangements poses another challenge.
- *Absence of priorities.* TILF may be diffusing efforts across too many issues. Certainly, measuring and comparing progress is vastly complicated by the quantity of commitments. However, we appreciate that setting clear priorities can be politically hazardous: APEC's most dramatic attempt to set trade priorities — the Early Voluntary Sectoral Liberalization (EVSL) initiative — proved overly ambitious and controversial. Still, it may be possible in some particularly complex issue areas, such as services, to adopt a building block approach by focusing on a few sub-sectors for a start, as suggested in the APIAN Issue Report on that subject. As an appropriate place to begin to apply consensus competition principles, the APIAN Issue Report on Competition and Regulatory Reform suggests that APEC should target hardcore cartels. The APIAN Issue Report on Tariffs proposes that APEC consider focusing on the elimination of tariff peaks and nuisance tariffs.
- *Shortfalls in member commitments.* IAPs often lack commitments that go beyond pre-existing Uruguay Round pledges. Many commitments also tend to be too general and vague for implementation, or to allow for evaluation. A respondent to an APIAN questionnaire on services stated: "The main impediment to implementation is that commitments are not clearly articulated in IAPs. For meaningful progress to be made, targets should be more clearly defined and achievements measured". In the area of investment policy, the APIAN Issue Report remarked that the current APEC member IAPs failed to address important impediments to foreign investment.
- *Weak evaluation procedures.* APEC member economies review their own performance and some now submit their IAPs to peer review, an innovation of potential value if made more rigorous. In 1999, the PECC undertook a study of IAPs, but its report was careful not to name individual APEC member economies. The lack of effective evaluation mechanisms deprives APEC of the sort of peer pressures that might foster better performance.

- *Dearth of specific APEC incentives.* APEC members suffer no consequences (beyond the damage to their own economic efficiency) for failure to table a strong IAP, or if implementation falls short of IAP commitments.
- *Insufficient political support for further liberalization.* Numerous respondents to APIAN survey questionnaires pointed out that the degree of government support for TILF was a critical variable in determining progress towards Bogor goals. Some respondents highlighted that private sector interest was a second important driver behind governments' behaviour. The reasons for official laxity vary across economies. Some APEC economies feel sufficiently burdened by the requirements of implementing their Uruguay Round commitments. Other economies, accustomed to tit-for-tat trade bargaining regimes, remain sceptical of voluntary unilateralism and hesitate to liberalize their trade regimes in the absence of specific reciprocity and more evident comparability. As noted by the APIAN Issue Report on Food and Agriculture, the reluctance of member economies to consider seriously liberalization in some key sectors undermines the credibility of their commitment to the Bogor goals.
- *Inadequate linkages with other international organizations.* A cross-cutting theme, according to APIAN Issue Reports, is that as a young regional organization, APEC has not established sufficiently strong linkages with existing international organizations. Some TILF working groups would benefit from deeper relations with counterpart WTO offices, as well as with the secretariats of other regional trading arrangements, and on labour-related matters, with the International Labour Organization (ILO). TILF working groups responsible for such areas as investment and competition policies would gain from stronger ties with the OECD and the United Nations Conference on Trade and Development (UNCTAD).

Recommendations on TILF

1. *APEC should clarify and prioritize some of its trade policy initiatives.* APEC could make more progress in some areas by updating its trade and investment agenda and by clarifying issue scope and coverage. In some complex issue areas, such as services and competition policy, APEC should consider prioritizing select sub-sectors, or actionable items. We also recommend that APEC establish priority areas for immediate progress in trade and investment liberalization, such as national treatment, non-tariff barriers and tariff peaks, and export subsidies. As has been done successfully with some facilitation measures, such priority goals

can be simultaneously pursued through integrated efforts utilizing both collective action plans (CAPs) and IAPs.

2. *APEC should continue to improve its IAPs.* Individual Action Plan commitments should be specific, concrete, and measurable to the extent possible. We look forward to the first fruits of the new electronic IAP format. There needs to be more precise identification of the non-tariff barriers (NTBs) to be removed and the steps by which their removal will take place. We endorse the recommendation in ABAC's 2000 Report that NTBs be treated more thoroughly in the IAPs.
3. *APEC members should be accountable for their IAP commitments.* We call upon APEC to establish effective mechanisms — both internal and external to APEC — for the review of members' IAP commitments and implementation. The IAP peer reviews should call for more rigorous commentaries. APEC should continue to call upon outside, independent experts to evaluate its TILF programmes; in the future, such evaluations should include member-specific assessments, in order to provide feedback, enhance comparability and confidence-building, and to exert peer pressure. For evaluation to be effective, however, IAP commitments would have to be more specific, measurable, and accompanied by a time frame. Clarification of benchmarks and end-points would also facilitate evaluation of individual member performance.

The core APEC principles of voluntary unilateralism preclude a comprehensive incentive regime. Nevertheless, we are persuaded that the establishment of effective and transparent systems to monitor the implementation of APEC's voluntary, non-binding commitments would not violate either the letter or the spirit of APEC principles, and could provide useful incentives for better performance.

Economic and Technical Cooperation (Ecotech)

APEC has been a pioneer in linking capacity-building to economic reform, and after the 1997-98 regional financial crisis, the developed economies more firmly grasped that both pillars of APEC — TILF and Ecotech — are indispensable to each other. We welcome this new consensus on the importance of capacity-building to economic development and national adaptation to globalization. Specifically, we are pleased that the design of the APEC Food System provides for a comprehensive integration of TILF and Ecotech elements.

The many Ecotech working groups have launched over 250 projects on a wide array of issues. The majority of these are "process" projects (such as conferences), training sessions, or database construction. APIAN believes that many of these Ecotech projects have value. Their relative "smallness" may be cost effective. Their lack of dramatic visibility is not necessarily a negative. In particular, building databases, as a means of organizing and disseminating information and promoting transparency and facilitating evaluation, is an appropriate function of an international organization. Training sessions are vital to capacity building and human resource development, and the APIAN Issue Report on that subject concluded that many APEC-approved human resource development (HRD) projects are well designed and innovative. The APIAN Issue Report on Energy found value in the innovative Implementation Facilitation Assistance Team (IFAT) programme, which sends joint public-private sector advisory teams to APEC member economies interested in reforming their energy sectors.

Ecotech is critical to the realization of APEC's vision and the economic development of its members. Yet, Ecotech suffers from a number of shortcomings that must be corrected if the current crisis of confidence in its programmes is to be overcome:

- *Excessive diffusion of limited resources.* APEC has recognized that Ecotech's scope is too diffuse, is shooting off into too many different areas at once and is guilty of duplication and overlap. APIAN research confirms this finding: for example, the Issue Report on Industrial Science and Technology noted that, in that area, there were too many *ad hoc* projects on a large variety of subjects. This tendency to want to be "all things to all people" is a common characteristic of multilateral organizations, especially those with weak institutionalization. Each APEC member economy has its pet projects which, when multiplied by 21, quickly accumulate into a laundry list. APEC has no effective executive committee or other authoritative mechanism for establishing firm priorities and for sorting through project proposals.
- *Proliferation of Ecotech forums.* Ecotech working groups, task forces and "networks" have multiplied over time. This proliferation leads to confusion and inefficiency, and makes it difficult to set priorities and to coordinate efforts.
- *Lack of coordination of defined APEC objectives.* The pursuit of APEC objectives at times requires a coordinated effort across a large number of Ecotech activities. APEC lacks the capacity to achieve the level of coordination required for effective implementation of such wide-ranging initiatives as the APEC Food System.

- *The Ecotech Subcommittee — an important innovation — lacks adequate authority.* To improve Ecotech coordination and efficiency, and to enhance public awareness of Ecotech success stories, APEC established the Ecotech Subcommittee (ESC). APIAN applauds this decision. Yet, the ESC lacks sufficient authority, resources, and tenure to realize fully its goals.
- *Many Ecotech initiatives are resource-starved.* A major constraint on Ecotech has been inadequate funding, especially for the poorer APEC members. The institution itself has minimal resources for Ecotech projects. APEC has not yet developed strong ties with existing multilateral lending agencies, such as the Asian Development Bank (ADB) and the World Bank, even though their boards of directors are controlled by many of the governments that are members of APEC. Nor has APEC devised adequate mechanisms for channelling bilateral sources into priority APEC projects.

Some observers have argued that APEC should approve and seek funding for one or several large, high-visibility projects, with a regional reach. We concur that Ecotech efforts should be more focused and much better funded. We note, for example, that the Panel of Independent Experts (offspring of the Eminent Person's Group) has proposed two major new initiatives to help APEC regain its vitality: the creation of an APEC Financial Institute endowed with a Brunei Fund of US$50–100 million; and consultations within APEC regarding the consistency of emerging subregional trading arrangements with APEC and WTO frameworks.

Recommendations on Ecotech

1. *APEC should overhaul its Ecotech programmes.* We share the consensus among official and outside observers that APEC needs to better focus its limited capacity to foster economic and technical cooperation. APEC needs to streamline Ecotech programmes, to set priorities, to rationalize working groups, and to improve coordination among Ecotech forums. We note the work of the management review committee, and consider that further reform efforts will be required. We believe it is time for a systematic overhaul of the organizational structure of Ecotech.

   To accomplish these reforms, APEC needs to develop more effective mechanisms to concentrate energies and to sort through project proposals. An APEC committee or working group should be given enhanced authority to scrutinize the labours of Ecotech working groups, to review proposed projects in accordance with APEC priorities, and to encourage coordination and avoid duplication. The Ecotech Subcommittee should be given more authority and resources to pursue its mandates, and should be given the jurisdiction to review Ecotech-related activities of TIFL working groups. The ESC's reliance on working groups and member economies to self-evaluate their performance incurs obvious limitations.

We welcome the recent decision by APEC Senior Officials to encourage independent, external reviews of Ecotech activities. To perform its evaluative role effectively, the ESC should be empowered and financed to commission independent, objective assessments of the overall organization of APEC's economic and technical cooperation, of the work of the various working groups, and of individual projects.

APEC also needs to find more funds for good Ecotech projects, better ways to disseminate the results of good programmes and more effective mechanisms for increasing its success stories.

2. *Ecotech needs more active funding.* APEC should make it a high priority to create an effective process that encourages the resource-rich multilateral development banks to fund sound Ecotech projects. More organic ties should also be pursued with bilateral donors. Private-sector involvement in specific projects should also be systematically encouraged. We suggest that consideration be given to establishing "Ecotech Funds", perhaps in collaboration with the Asian Development Bank, that would use APEC creativity to catalyze financial support from these public and private sources behind APEC priorities. We welcome the recent initiative to allow TILF funds to be used for worthy Ecotech projects.
3. *APEC should mandate action plans for Ecotech.* Individual and collective action plans should be prepared for Ecotech. To assure coherence and succinctness, such action plans should be restricted to APEC-specific programmes and projects. In their IAPs, members should specify both commitments and implementation results, and include timetables and quantifiable targets to the extent possible. Member economies should break their action plans into short and medium/long-term components. Where possible, the linkage between Ecotech and TILF action plans should be noted. Member economies should submit their Ecotech IAPs to APEC's senior officials, which would refer them to the ESC for review. To ensure transparency, the ESC should prepare a standardized, user-friendly format for the action plans.

APEC as an Institution

As we remarked at the outset, APEC's "soft institutionalism" is a natural outgrowth of the historical circumstances of its birth. In many ways, the level, breath and intensity of APEC activities and forums are impressive. We can perceive a community of spirit emerging among the thousands of officials who meet their agency counterparts at APEC-sponsored meetings. We find that the annual Leaders' Meetings serve multiple purposes and ought to be continued. But as the Issue Report on APEC as an Institution stresses, APEC will fall well short of its goals if it does not find a better match between its aspirations and its institutional structures.

For some years, APEC itself has recognized that its efforts are too diffuse and that its bureaucracy has suffered from over-extension. Yet calls for rationalization have proven largely ineffective. We believe that centrifugal forces will continue to pull APEC in too many directions unless and until APEC confronts some critical institutional matters.

While we believe that it is vital for APEC to confront its institutional sprawl, we do not claim to have all the answers to these complex bureaucratic problems, which at their root are profoundly political in nature. In this spirit of humility, we offer these reform proposals.

Recommendations on Institutional Structures

1. *The APEC Secretariat should be strengthened.* Currently, the very small Secretariat in Singapore is composed of officials temporarily on loan from member governments and whose primary responsibilities are to help organize logistics and manage paper flow. A stronger Secretariat that has more in-house capacity to monitor implementation of APEC initiatives can help the institution to better evaluate, rationalize, and coordinate both TIFL and Ecotech. As the APIAN Issue Report on Human Resource Development suggested, the Secretariat could also serve as a communications hub in the flow of information within APEC forums and between APEC projects and outside organizations and civil society.

   To strengthen the Secretariat, we propose the creation of longer-term professional positions, as well as the multi-year secondment of substantive expertise from member governments. We judge that one-year rotations do not allow for continuity and leadership, and so we also suggest the designation of a Secretary-General with a multi-year term of office. We note that ASEAN strengthened its Secretariat in Jakarta in both of these aspects during the 1990s. We do not believe that such limited reforms would create an expensive or overbearing bureaucracy; but they could help APEC to make better use of its resources.

2. *APEC should deepen its ties with other international and regional organizations.* Such relations can promote policy consistency and convergence, facilitate access to expertise and finance, and help to disseminate awareness of APEC's success stories. We cite as a positive example the ties that APEC's financial and corporate governance forums have with the IMF and the OECD. As noted earlier, we urge Ecotech to seek financial and technical support from multilateral development banks that share APEC objectives. TILF forums should deepen their relations with the WTO, the OECD, and other relevant multilateral forums. APEC should consult more routinely with other regional trade arrangements, such that their gains in liberalization are constructively nested under APEC.
3. *Ministries of Finance should be better integrated into the APEC process.* Traditionally, the region's strong finance ministries viewed APEC as dominated by other governmental entities (ministries of foreign affairs and trade, offices of prime ministers and presidents), and hence sought to keep APEC at arms length. Prior to the Asian financial crisis, APEC analysed macroeconomic trends but did not tackle most financial matters. The post-financial crisis agenda, however, demands that APEC better integrate finance and development. Ecotech training now includes issues like financial market regulation and corporate governance, and TILF investment and competition forums are focusing on financial markets. In response to these new realities, finance ministerials are now integrated into the overall APEC schedule, and the APEC central fund has approved projects involving finance ministries, but the respondents to the APIAN issue questionnaires on finance agreed that APEC can do more. While the questionnaires found no consensus on many of the more controversial issues regarding global financial reform, respondents did approve of APEC's greater focus on financial consultations, information sharing, training, and other Ecotech-related activities.
4. *Partnerships with outside groups should be strengthened.* APEC has pioneered close relations with the private sector, through the formation of ABAC and the CEO Forum, and as the APIAN Issue Reports underscore, active private sector participation in such specific initiatives as in energy (through the Energy Working Group Business Partnership) and quality control (through the APEC Experts and Trainers Executive Workshop on International Quality Assurance Systems, or IQAS). These examples of APEC outreach could be multiplied with others in the private sector as well as with other non-governmental groups interested in participating in APEC working groups and in specific

projects. APIAN questionnaires suggest that strong business and civil society participation contributes to the successful implementation of APEC initiatives. We endorse the recommendation in the *1998 APEC Senior Officials Report on Ecotech* that business be involved in all stages of the project cycle. We concur with the recommendation in ABAC's 2000 Report that sectoral government-business dialogues promote APEC's facilitation agenda. We welcome China's convocation of a major conference in 2001 to encourage private sector participation in human resource development.

We believe that NGO involvement with select working groups, such as those responsible for the environment, human resource development, gender equality and micro-enterprises, would be particularly beneficial.

5. *Academic engagement should be encouraged.* To help build a broadly based Pacific community of intellectuals, APEC should reach out more systematically to universities and policy institutes. Researchers can contribute their expertise and analytical skills to many APEC forums. In particular, at the 1993 Seattle Leaders' Meeting, APEC launched the APEC Study Centres, to promote research, dissemination and regional cooperation. APIAN — as a voluntary grouping of APEC Study Centres — is convinced that APEC can take better advantage of the Centres' capacities and goodwill.
6. *APEC should augment its dissemination efforts.* APIAN questionnaires revealed a stunning lack of public awareness, even among experts, of APEC activities. To build wider support for its activities, to catalyze replication of its success stories, and to promote transparency and constructive feedback, APEC needs to substantially improve its dissemination and outreach. APEC's problems are not merely ones of public relations, but better information flow is part of the solution. A better-staffed Secretariat should devote more resources to dissemination and outreach to non-governmental groups. We urge the Secretariat to continue to improve its webpage and for APEC to make better use of information technology (IT) in various programmes, especially in human resource development. We welcome the launching of the Ecotech clearing house, and advise that it be expanded and continually updated. Broader and more systematic engagement with the private sector and other non-governmental groups would be an important component of an energized effort to broaden APEC's base. It is only through deep and broad dialogue that APEC can realize its core mission — to foster a community of nations and peoples in the Asia-Pacific.

THE APIAN ISSUE REPORTS

In the preparation of this comprehensive Policy Report, APIAN researchers produced separate reports on the following issues: tariffs, services, investment policy, competition and regulatory reform, mobility of business people, human resource development, food and agriculture, industrial science and technology, energy, corporate governance, finance, and on APEC as an institution. In addition, we included a survey on certain trade facilitation measures conducted by a participating APEC Study Centre. A list of the APIAN Issue Coordinators can be found in the appendix. A compendium of the Issue Reports is presented in Section II in this volume.

We summarize the main findings of these Issue Reports, with an emphasis on recommendations for improving APEC performance.

Tariffs

Many of the APEC economies have been slashing their tariffs; however, it is methodologically impossible to assign these gains to APEC as opposed to other catalysts to liberalization, such as the GATT/WTO, the international financial institutions, and endogenous domestic pressures.

More clearly attributable to APEC is the enhanced transparency of tariff regimes under the improving IAP formats. By requiring members to report actual and planned improvements, the new electronic formats have greatly improved the comparability of individual data sets. The new format could provide quantitative indicators on the progress towards policy objectives.

The Issue Report also found that the strength of government support for tariff liberalization has been a critical variable in determining the value of the IAPs. Attitudes of business and other interest groups have also been influential.

To enhance the visible value-added contribution of APEC to tariff reduction, the Issue Report suggested that APEC should consider focusing on the elimination of tariff peaks and nuisance tariffs.

Services

The Issue Report's analysis of the IAP commitments in services found that of the 264 short-term commitments, 97 per cent were implemented. IAPs contain far fewer longer-term commitments. Some developed economies that already have low barriers to trade in services have few or no commitments in the IAPs.

IAPs have not been clear and precise in presenting information on commitments on services. It is not adequate, for example, to state that financial services will be liberalized. Commitments should include time-frames for implementation and indicate whether or not commitments are part of the WTO negotiations.

There is a need for greater dialogue among government officials, businesses, and interest groups within economies, to assure support for the timely implementation of commitments. Ultimately, strong government support is critical to successful implementation.

Investment Policy

Significant progress has been made in implementing the collective actions aimed at achieving the Bogor goal of free and open investment. Completed projects under the Collective Action Plans (CAPs) on Investment include enhanced transparency through the publication of the *APEC Investment Guidebook*; policy dialogue that developed, in conjunction with the business sector, a menu of options for investment liberalization and related business facilitation for inclusion in IAPs; and economic and technical cooperation through a series of seminars and training programmes.

However, the Issue Report cautioned that the contribution of these collective actions towards achieving the Bogor goal had yet to be evaluated, and called for an assessment of the impact of these collective actions.

Data from eight APEC economies revealed that most of the economies complied with almost all of the twelve principles listed in APEC's Non-Binding Investment Principles (NBIP). However, none of the eight economies had yet complied with all of the twelve principles.

At least in some cases, the current IAPs and CAPs will not be sufficient to assure attainment of the Bogor goals, as additional impediments to foreign investment exist. Therefore, the Issue Report recommended that IAPs include a more complete inventory on investment impediments, as a means of exerting pressure to accelerate liberalization. IAPs should also include investment-related initiatives undertaken unilaterally, such as privatization and reduction of ownership restrictions.

Competition and Regulatory Reform

The Issue Report noted that although APEC's competition principles were quite limited substantively, they nevertheless provided an important framework in which to promote best practices and gradual convergence over time. APEC's principles do go beyond the WTO and OECD work currently under way.

Measures should be developed with regard to some practices to ensure that policies and approaches are converging over time. Approaches to hardcore cartels may be an appropriate subject for developing more substantive non-binding principles.

An APEC database on competition policies should include information on related topics, and best practices should be compiled and analysed.

APEC should seek more business engagement and promote greater collaboration with other international organizations active in this area.

Mobility of Business People

Only eight economies had joined the APEC Business Travel Card system by mid-2000. The system seeks to expedite the freer movement of business people throughout the region by offering accredited business travellers visa-free travel and faster airport processing.

Reasons for the lack of participation by other APEC members, especially the more developed economies, include security concerns and labour market protection. A more secure Business Travel Card is being proposed. The Issue Report suggests that since short-term migration poses less of a threat to domestic employment and is more generally accepted than long-term residency, APEC should focus on the former.

More broadly, the Issue Report found that, unless travel and migration processes were streamlined and standardized across economies, the initiative to enhance business mobility would at best be slow and halting. Therefore, APEC should seek agreement for codes and standards on travel and migration regulations and processes among its members. Most importantly, APEC should recognize the labour mobility programmes already in place in select APEC members, and should seek to expand them throughout APEC. Specifically, APEC should explore short-term visa-free travel, taking into account the special circumstances of each member. APEC should study ASEAN's practices in this area.

Trade Facilitation

(Summary of a "Survey on Customs, Standards and Business Mobility in the APEC Region," a report prepared by the Asia-Pacific Foundation of Canada for the APEC Business Advisory Council, July, 2000)

This questionnaire survey of business people in the APEC region confirmed the importance they attribute to pursuing trade facilitation measures in the area of customs, standards and business mobility, and validates APEC's traditional emphasis on facilitation issues.

Survey respondents from developed and developing APEC member economies alike considered trade facilitation issues to be among the most important trade impediments in the region. Customs procedures, in particular, were ranked as the most serious trade impediments, even more so than restrictive administrative regulations and tariffs. This view was especially pronounced in the case of developing economy respondents. Issues with regard to standards were ranked somewhat lower, but nearly 40 per cent of respondents nevertheless considered standards-related trade impediments to be very serious or serious.

The survey also raised serious questions about the effectiveness of APEC implementation. In each of the three facilitation areas, respondents were asked to reflect on specific APEC initiatives or on APEC's effectiveness in those areas generally. The response was overwhelmingly negative — respondents were either unaware of APEC's efforts or they felt APEC's efforts were not effective. This result is a serious rebuke to APEC, whether interpreted as lack of action, lack of success, or simply a lack of communication.

Human Resource Development (HRD)

The scope of HRD activities has expanded substantially since the founding of APEC in 1989 but resources directed to HRD have not kept pace. This limits the contribution of HRD as a catalyst within the APEC process.

Because it cuts across so much of what APEC strives to accomplish through Ecotech, HRD capacity-building is embedded in a wide range of initiatives and projects. To this end, HRD requires a strong emphasis on building networks to share and coordinate efforts where there is an HRD component, as well as to generate effective input from individuals and organizations outside APEC.

The participation of the private sector is one area where HRD has much further to go to achieve its potential as a catalyst for broader capacity-building. One successful positive example of important private sector participation is the APEC Experts-Trainers-Executives Workshops on International Quality Assurance Systems (IQAS); seventeen workshops were conducted in nine APEC economies, with participation from over 500 private sector organizations.

The Issue Report concluded that APEC should improve its capacity to share the results of its successful efforts. HRD projects should be better linked to the world outside of APEC meetings and agendas if they are to have real impact. The special role of APEC needs to be emphasized in assessing the APEC value-added of HRD projects.

Food and Agriculture

In 1999 APEC Leaders instructed ministers and officials to implement a set of recommendations on establishing the APEC Food System — a visionary and far-reaching concept that calls for an integrated approach involving both TILF and Ecotech elements.

Some APEC forums, notably the Agriculture Technical Cooperation Experts Group and Standards and Conformance Subcommittee, have been able to adapt and expand existing programmes in order to respond to the Leaders' instruction, although it is too early to assess their effectiveness. The Infrastructure Workshop has, in conjunction with the PECC Food and Agriculture Forum, initiated a promising initiative known as RISE (Regional Integration for Sustainable Economies) and two RISE pilot projects have reportedly met considerable success. The APIAN Issue Report proposed that APEC now consider whether and in what form the RISE initiative should be further developed to form an integral part of APEC Food System implementation. However, we were unable to find evidence that APEC is actively considering the possible further development of RISE, and no budgetary provision appears to have been made beyond the current year.

More disturbing still is that we were unable to locate information indicating a substantial response to the Leaders' instruction by a number of other relevant forums. The APIAN Report also found that APEC currently lacks provision for the kind of coordination across the relevant forums that will be needed to implement the Ecotech-related aspects of the APEC Food System.

In the light of the agreed Bogor goals and principles of the Osaka Action Agenda, the APIAN Issue Report found it puzzling that in relation to trade, the APEC Food System recommendations refer to trade promotion rather than trade liberalization. This stance apparently reflects resistance by some APEC members to the use of the term "liberalization" in relation to trade in food products.

The APIAN Issue Report concluded that APEC must urgently review the state of implementation of the APEC Food System, identify the gaps, and make credible provisions for more effective implementation in the future.

Industrial Science and Technology (IST)

The Issue Report gave higher marks to the achievements related to the exchange of technical and scientific information and participation in international projects. It also evaluated positively the advances made in HRD activities. However, progress was judged to be mediocre in the areas of government–business relations, participation in international technological partnerships, and exchange of technical and scientific personnel. With regard to progress in regulatory frameworks, results were mixed, ranging from significant to irrelevant, depending on the reporting economy. The Report also found that participation in IST was concentrated among a few economies.

The most important weaknesses underlying the IST initiatives were: lack of business interest in APEC IST activities; the diversity of membership of APEC that made it difficult for many members to discover value in IST projects; and the insufficiency of resources to support wider participation of member economies and institutions.

The Issue Report recommended that APEC should find ways to increase business interest, in particular by using the IST Working Group meetings as an opportunity for increased interaction. The Report also proposed that APEC should coordinate more effectively science and technology activities that were initiated by several working groups. In order to provide more focus and structure to the IST programme, APEC should select one (or a limited number) of focal themes of activity for each year (or multi-year period).

Energy

During the last decade, the APEC Energy Working Group (EWG) played a leading role in the collection of data on energy supply and demand, in energy research and in policy development. The Issue Report found that the establishment of the Asia-Pacific Energy Research Centre in collaboration with the government of Japan, as well as the completion of a series of research projects by the expert groups, have added significantly to the understanding of energy issues in the region. The EWG's development of the fourteen non-binding principles for rational energy consumption has given impetus to the development of energy policies in member economies. More recently, the initiation in the private sector of Implementation Facilitation Assistance Teams (IFATs) to visit member economies and assist in the joint development of energy policies and programmes, has been a major advance — highlighting the role that APEC can play in policy formulation and implementation.

Major factors behind the EWG's successes include: the sustained high-level support of a member government (Australia); continuity in the leadership of the EWG; institutionalization of research capacity; and the strong emphasis on high-level creative partnerships with the private sector.

Corporate Governance

Weakness in corporate governance has been identified as a major contributor to the 1997–98 financial crises in some Asian countries. Finance ministers have recognized that APEC can play a useful role in several areas including: the design of more effective regulatory practices at the national level; the implementation of reform at the company level, to promote better standards in accountancy, transparency, and reporting;

and the development of governance skills in both the public and private sectors. So far, in this new area, APEC has begun with a focus on problem definition and statements of general principles, and must now give attention to issues of implementation.

Finance

The experts responding to the APIAN questionnaire on financial stability presented no consensus on the more controversial proposals for international financial reform. However, most respondents advocated a stronger role for APEC in this area, especially since most believe that APEC has hitherto contributed very little in terms of concrete results. For example, no expert believed that APEC has yet played an effective role in promoting safe, sustainable capital flows in the region. As respondents generally opined that global financial institutions have been either ineffective or downright destructive, there would appear to be a role for APEC as a regional institution — as a complement to (perhaps reformed) global institutions — in confronting the myriad problems associated with financial stability.

APEC was not originally conceived of as a "financial" organization. In the wake of the 1997–98 regional financial crisis, APEC has placed a stronger emphasis on financial matters in general, and financial stability in particular. Nevertheless, most respondents underscored the need to do more — to improve consultation, information sharing, training, and other Ecotech-related activities, with resources to support them. Respondents also gave priority to enhancing financial-crisis management, by pooling resources in APEC, promoting currency stability and coordination and replicating some of the capacities of the OECD.

APEC as an Institution

The main conclusions of this report appear in the body of the Report.

APPENDIX A

SIGNATORIES

Signatories are listed in alphabetical order by member economy, with institutional affiliation provided for identification purposes only.

Australia

John McKay
Director
Australian APEC Study Centre
and Monash Asia Institute
Monash University

Canada

Yuen Pau Woo
Director
Asia-Pacific Foundation of Canada

Chile

Manfred Wilhemy
Executive Director
Chile-Pacific Foundation

People's Republic of China

Lu Jianren
Deputy Director
APEC Policy Research Centre
Chinese Academy of Social Sciences (CASS)
Institute of Asia-Pacific Studies

Hong Kong, China

Ku Wai Li
Coordinator
APEC Study Centre
City University of Hong Kong

Japan

Neantro Saavedra-Rivano
Director
APEC Study Centre
University of Tsukuba

Toshihisa Toyoda
Professor
APEC Study Centre
Kobe University

New Zealand

Robert Scollay
Director
APEC Study Centre
University of Auckland

Philippines

Myrna Austria
Director
Philippine APEC Study Centre Network Secretariat
Philippine Institute for Development Studies

Leonardo A. Lanzona
Chair
Economics Department
Ateneo de Manila University

Singapore

Chia Siow Yue
Director
APEC Study Centre, and
Director
Institute of Southeast Asian Studies (ISEAS)

South Korea

Hyungdo Ahn
Executive Director
APEC National Study Centre
Korean Institute for International Economic Policy (KIEP)

Honggue Lee
Professor
Konkuk University

Chinese Taipei

Rong-I Wu
Executive Director
Chinese Taipei APEC Study Centre
President
Taiwan Institute of Economic Research (TIER)

Chen-Sheng Ho
Associate Research Fellow
Chinese Taipei APEC Study Centre
Taiwan Institute of Economic Research

Thailand
Medhi Krongkaew
Director
Thai APEC Study Centre (TASC)
Institute of East Asian Studies
Thammasat University

United States of America
Vinod Aggarwal
Director
Berkeley APEC Study Center (BASC)
University of California, Berkeley

Richard E. Feinberg
Director
APEC Study Center
Graduate School of International Relations and Pacific Studies (IR/PS)
University of California, San Diego

Merit E. Janow
Co-Director
APEC Study Center
Columbia University

Hugh Patrick
Co-Director
APEC Study Center
Columbia University

Raul Hinojosa-Ojeda
Director
North American Integration and Development Center
University of California, Los Angeles

Michael G. Plummer
Associate Professor
Graduate School of International Economics
Brandeis University

APPENDIX B

EXECUTIVE COMMITTEE OF THE APEC INTERNATIONAL ASSESSMENT NETWORK (APIAN)

Richard Feinberg (Project Coordinator), Graduate School of International Relations and Pacific Studies, University of California, San Diego.
Hyungdo Ahn, Korea Institute for International Economic Policy, South Korea.
Myrna Austria, Philippine Institute for Development Studies, Philippines
John McKay, Monash Asia Institute, Monash University, Australia.
Neantro Saavedra-Rivano, Graduate School of International Political Economy, University of Tsukuba, Japan.
Robert Scollay, University of Auckland, New Zealand.
Manfred Wilhelmy, Chile-Pacific Foundation, Chile.
Rong-I Wu, Taiwan Institute of Economic Research, Chinese Taipei.

APPENDIX C

Tariffs

Honggue Lee
Konkuk University
South Korea

Services

Chen-Sheng Ho
APEC Study Centre
Taiwan Institute of Economic Research
Chinese Taipei

Investment Policy

Myrna Austria
Director
Philippine APEC Study Centre Network Secretariat
Philippine Institute for Development Studies
Philippines

Competition and Regulatory Reform

Merit E. Janow
Co-Director
APEC Study Center
Columbia University
USA

APIAN ISSUE COORDINATORS

Mobility of Business People

Leonardo Lanzona
Chair
Economics Department
Ateneo de Manila University
Philippines

Human Resource Development

Jianren Lu
Deputy Director
Institute of Asia-Pacific Studies
Chinese Academy of Social Sciences
China

Glen Taylor
Deputy Director
APEC Study Center
College of Business Administration
University of Hawaii at Manoa
USA

Food and Agriculture

Robert Scollay
Director
APEC Study Centre
University of Auckland
New Zealand

Industrial Science and Technology

Neantro Saavedra-Rivano
Director
APEC Study Centre
Graduate School of International Political Economy
University of Tsukuba
Japan

Energy

John McKay
Director
Australian APEC Study Centre and Monash Asia Institute
Monash University
Australia

Corporate Governance

John McKay
Director
Australian APEC Study Centre and Monash Asia Institute
Monash University
Australia

Finance

Peter Petri
Dean
Graduate School of International Economics and Finance
Brandeis University
USA

Michael G. Plummer
Associate Professor
Graduate School of International Economics
Brandeis University
USA

APEC as an Institution

Vinod K. Aggarwal
Director

Kun-Chin Lin
Project Director
Berkeley APEC Study Center (BASC)
University of California, Berkeley
USA

SECTION II
ISSUE REPORTS

2

IAP COMMITMENTS IN SERVICES

Chen-Sheng Ho

Introduction

The idea for the establishment of the APEC International Assessment Network (APIAN) became a reality on 28–30 January 1999, when leaders of APEC Study Centres met in La Jolla, California (Feinberg 1999c, p. 1). The rationale for the creation of APIAN was the non-existence of comprehensive effort that was independent of governments for the purpose of tracking and evaluating the implementation of APEC work. It has been almost impossible to conclude whether there has been progress from "words to deeds". The lack of information has prevented the scholarly community and civil society from having a clear understanding of APEC. Therefore, they are largely unappreciative of and sceptical towards APEC. The lack of transparency and public debate could cause inertia among APEC officials to act upon official promises. Without the input of scholars and external experts, APEC is deprived of important sources of expert information and valuable feedback (Feinberg 1999a, p. 1).

APIAN is a cooperative project composed of several APEC Study Centres. The project has identified five major issue areas for analysis:

1) Trade and Investment and Business Facilitation; 2) Economic and Technical Cooperation; 3) Financial Stability; 4) Participation; and 5) Organizational Structures. The five issue areas are further divided into several parts (Feinberg 1999b, pp. 1–2). The goal is to increase knowledge among government officials, the general public, scholars, and businesses on the various APEC activities. APIAN seeks to encourage the accomplishment of APEC objectives and commitments. In addition, the project strives to recommend ways for APEC to improve its work progress (Feinberg 1999c, p. 1).

The Chinese Taipei APEC Study Centre (CTASC) at the Taiwan Institute of Economic Research has committed itself to be a participant of APIAN. The CTASC has chosen the issue of trade in services as part of its contribution to APIAN. Trade in Services has been chosen for study because APEC members are concerned with the pace of services' liberalization. This issue area is not only important to APEC but also to the World Trade Organization (WTO).

The main objective of the project for the CTASC is to analyse the progress that all APEC members have made in implementing their commitments in the services' section of the Individual Action Plans (IAPs). The IAPs contain APEC members' plans for reaching the Bogor objective of free trade and investment by 2010 for developed economies and 2020 for developing economies. Every APEC member has written an IAP that is updated annually. Specifically, the Coordinator of the study will evaluate whether or not APEC members' implementation of their commitments in IAPs is on schedule.

This chapter consists of four main sections. The first is the introduction to the project. The second provides the background information on APEC activities in the area of trade in services. A review of research on services is also discussed in this section. The evaluation of APEC's commitments in services, as presented in the IAPs, is the main focus of the third section. This section includes the discussion of the methodology used to analyse APEC members' commitments in services, and the results of the evaluation. Finally, recommendations are stated.

Background Information

APEC Activities in Services

The APEC Committee on Trade and Investment expressed the need to form the Group on Services (GOS) in order to allow for greater attention to the important issue of services. As a result, GOS began to work on trade in services when it held its first meeting on 31 January 1997. During the meeting, members agreed that GOS should continue to focus on the work that APEC had done in services. In addition, GOS should focus on gathering and analysing information, sharing experience, and maintaining transparency. Particularly, the Group noted the need to receive feedback from businesses (APEC 1997a).

The second meeting of GOS on 18 May 1997 in Quebec, Canada, provided more details on the work programme. Members were cognizant of the importance of IAPs. Thus, they decided to continually review the IAPs. Furthermore, members discussed the general issue of trade in services, on ways for studying the issue on the basis of the negative or positive list approach. GOS further related the need to identify measures affecting trade in services and the meaning of free and open trade in the services sector. The Canadian delegation gave a presentation of issues affecting the measurement of trade in services (APEC 1997b, pp. 1–2).

The above paragraphs relate some of the major activities of GOS at the beginning of its existence. As one can infer, the work programme of GOS is extremely broad, as it studies issues related to trade in services. Recently, GOS has continued to maintain its comprehensive approach. One of the most important work for GOS in the year 2000 was to give input on the services portion of the electronic IAP (E-IAP). The creation of E-IAP is of great importance to APEC. Members have noted that the E-IAP should not utilize the same classification as the GATS (General Agreement on Trade in Services) and should not just list restrictions as GATS commitment schedules. Economies could provide as much information as possible through hyper-links to the E-IAP (APEC 2000a, pp. 1-2).

GOS is in the process of developing a broader policy framework for APEC's work on services. The Committee on Trade and Investment (CTI) has requested GOS to produce a service agenda for APEC that will enhance the coordination of all service work. The establishment of a mechanism for maintaining working relationships with other forums is under discussion. This effort is particularly important to GOS, as services cover a wide area. The development of a menu of options for voluntary liberalization and facilitation of service trade and investment is another noteworthy work of GOS. The menu of options is composed of three main parts: 1) Liberalization; 2) Facilitation; and 3) Economic and Technical Cooperation. Liberalization consists of measures that affect most-favoured-nation (MFN) treatment, national treatment, and market access. Measures could come from the IAPs and services schedules of members. Facilitation measures include transparency, regulatory principles, mutual recognition, and competition principles. Economic and Technical Cooperation encompasses measures for improving the utilization of contact points, technical assistance, and training (APEC 2000a, pp. 2-3).

Activities stated here only cover some of the wide range of work that GOS has accomplished since its establishment. For those who are interested in knowing more about the work of GOS, the APEC website provides a comprehensive coverage.

Review of Research on Services in APEC

Several studies have been undertaken in the area of trade in services since the APEC Manila Action Plan for APEC (MAPA), which includes Collective Action Plans (CAPs) and IAPs. Findlay and Warren (1999) have presented a study that relates the various ways to measure barriers to services trade and investment in "Impediments to Services Sector Trade and Investment." According to the authors, they have identified five methods: 1) sectoral case studies; 2) examination of commitments to reform in the APEC IAP process; 3) assessment of the frequency of occurrence of impediments; 4) estimation of indicators of restrictiveness; and 5) general equilibrium modelling.

Since this chapter is primarily concerned with APEC trade in services, it would be appropriate to relate both authors' views on assessing the CAPs and IAPs. They state that IAPs furnish different information in relation to GATS. Generally, IAPs list APEC members' commitments that will be implemented, while the GATS provides information on completed commitments. In addition, the authors point out that some commitments in IAPs contain more information and cover more activities than others. They further relate that the IAPs can show the extent to which barriers to services are removed in each APEC economy. One can review the IAPs to find out whether commitments have been implemented and whether members have moved further from their original commitments. Another method calls for analysing the extent to which additional liberalization is needed to achieve the Bogor objectives of free trade and investment. This means identifying liberalizing measures that are not stated in CAPs and IAPs (Findlay and Warren 1999, pp. 8–10).

After a careful examination of Findlay and Warren's paper, it can be noted that they have presented a broad range of methods to analyse impediments to trade in services and investment. The methods mentioned could serve as a guide for researchers to study barriers to services trade in APEC. The methods could generally be classified under the positive or negative list approach. In the study of trade in services, identifying the actions leading to liberalization is considered the positive list method. On the other hand, the examination of barriers is linked to the negative list method.

Findlay and Warren (1999) have provided us with an overview of the various methods for analysing trade in services. We will now focus our attention on a scholar who is considered a pioneer in the assessment of the APEC economies' ability to achieve the Bogor objectives. Ever since the creation of MAPA, which consists of CAPs and IAPs, researchers have been interested in knowing whether APEC members could achieve the Bogor objectives. The publication of *APEC's Progress Toward the Bogor Target: A Quantitative Assessment of Individual Action Plans* by Yamazawa (1997) has given us valuable insight on the subject of IAP evaluation.

Since we are concerned here with APEC's work on trade in services, this chapter will review Yamazawa's appraisal of this issue. According to Yamazawa (1997), most APEC members have stated in their IAPs the current position and plans for liberalizing services trade using the positive list approach. The economies mention commitments to liberalization, and not impediments. The author believes that in order to assess the ability of the IAPs to achieve the Bogor objectives, it is necessary to analyse impediments to services trade. Thus, the GATS Commitment Table is utilized to identify impediments to trade in services for the APEC economies. The study, however, only focuses on four sectors: 1) telecommunications; 2) tourism; 3) transport (air, land, and marine); and 4) energy. The outcome of the analysis consists of grading each economy with a numerical score. An economy's score is based on the current position and future plans for liberalization. The evaluation shows that the United States has the highest score (Yamazawa 1997, pp. 28–30). This means that the United States is the most open economy in trade in services, and in the best position to reach the Bogor objectives.

Yamazawa and Urata (1999) have given us an updated version of the aforementioned landmark assessment, in "Trade and Investment Liberalization and Facilitation." In the new study, the authors use the 1998 IAPs for reference. They relate that high barriers exist in several service sectors. There is a dearth of information on the impediments. Ways to reduce the restrictions remain to be studied. It will be up to the new round of WTO negotiations. The authors are unsure of the extent to which liberalization in services would be accomplished under the voluntary method of liberalization in IAPs. In addition, the result of the analysis shows that the United States continues to receive the highest score in trade in services (Yamazawa and Urata 1999, pp. 14–16).

The Pacific Economic Cooperation Council (PECC) has recently published *Assessing APEC Individual Action Plans and their Contribution to APEC's Goals*. According to the PECC (1999), the APEC economies have not met the guidelines for drawing up the IAPs, as stated in the Osaka Action Agenda (OAA). Examples abound where economies have not made any commitments. Some of the commitments cannot be monitored because of insufficient information provided in the IAPs.

In addition, statements of implementation cannot be linked with earlier statements of intent. The study further notes that there exist cases of commitments that are not stated in the IAPs. The overall assessment is that the IAPs contain an abundance of details which are not really useful (PECC 1999, pp. 43-44).

The study further posits that the services section of the IAPs is disappointing because of the many details needed to satisfy the reporting guidelines for services of the OAA. The guidelines request the economies to give a full negative list, which is beyond the capacity of the WTO process. The PECC has stated the value of the negative list approach. The lack of useful details could be an indication of the difficulties in achieving the objectives of providing a full negative list (PECC 1999, p. 53).

Evaluation of Progress

Methodology

The purpose of this section is to describe the methodology that has been chosen to evaluate the extent to which APEC member economies have implemented the commitments discussed in the IAPs. The first step of the evaluation process has been to list the necessary sources of information for analysis. APEC economies have annually distributed three different publications: 1) *Individual Action Plans (IAPs)*; 2) *Summary of Specific Changes (SSCs) vis-à-vis the Last Version of the IAP*; and 3) *Summary of Individual Action Plans (SIAPs)*. The IAPs contain detailed information on members' commitments and other pertinent information. The SSCs specifically relate information about previous commitments achieved, new commitments, and other revisions. The SIAPs focus on stating information regarding the time-frame for completion of commitments. It must be noted that the SSCs and the SIAPs are also known by other names. The SSCs have been called Summary of Implementation and Improvements. The SIAPs are also known as Matrix of Individual Action Plans. The IAPs, SSCs, and SIAPs are available at the APEC Secretariat website.

The second step has been to locate all the commitments of the APEC economies from the three aforementioned publications, from 1996 to 1999. The commitments are classified under twelve major categories of services stated in the IAPs: 1) business; 2) communication and related engineering; 3) construction; 4) distribution; 5) educational; 6) environmental; 7) financial; 8) health-related and social; 9) tourism and travel-related; 10) recreational, cultural, and sporting; 11) transport; and 12) energy. Since the commitments contain information on the time-frame for completion, the commitments are further grouped under short-term or medium/long-term. The short-term was for commitments with a deadline of 2000, while the medium/long-term is for a completion date that ranges from 2001 to 2010/2020. The ending date coincides with the deadline for the Bogor objectives of 2010 for developed economies, and 2020 for developing economies.

The final step has been to construct four tables that list the commitments of the APEC economies, beginning with 1996, 1997, 1998, and 1999. The tables contain information on the number of commitments of each country within a particular category of services and time-frame. In addition, information on the completion status of the commitments is also given in the tables. A "yes" next to the number of commitments indicates completion, while a "no" signifies an ongoing implementation process. Thus, the tables provide data that allow us to determine whether or not APEC members have implemented their commitments in IAPs.

Outcome of Evaluation

After a careful analysis of APEC economies' commitments, the important finding was that members for the most part have completed the implementation of their commitments within the stated time-frame. In the case of short-term commitments with a deadline of 2000, one can see from the tables that members have acted upon their commitments, as indicated by "yes" next to the number of commitments (see Tables 1,2,3, and 4). The total number of short-term commitments was 264, with only 2 short-term commitments yet to be implemented. This means a completion rate of 99 per cent. The tables indicate that the economies emphasize short-term commitments, given the larger number relative to medium/long-term commitments. Chinese Taipei has not implemented 2 commitments, pending its entry into the WTO.

In the case of medium/long-term commitments, the deadline is still some way off. In total, there are 38 medium/long-term commitments. The tables show us that the economies have not implemented medium/long-term commitments in advance of the deadline. These commitments would most likely be completed on time, given that the economies have adhered to the deadline set for short-term commitments.

When Table 5 is examined, the most important finding is that some categories of services have more commitments than others. In terms of the total number of short-term implemented commitments, the economies have stated the most commitments in communications and related engineering services, with a figure of 79. Financial services follow closely behind with a total of 71 short-term completed commitments. APEC

TABLE 1 **1996 IAP Commitments in Services of APEC Economies**

Services	Australia		Brunei		Canada		Chile		PRC		HK, China		Indonesia		Japan		Korea		Malaysia	
	ST	MTLT	ST	MTLT	ST	MTLT	ST	MTLT	ST	MTLT	ST	MTLT	ST	MTLT	ST	MTLT	ST	MTLT	ST	MTI
Business	5Yes										2Yes				1Yes		2Yes		1Yes	
Communica-tion & Related Engineering	3Yes		1Yes						1Yes		6Yes				3Yes		2Yes	1No		
Construction																	1Yes			
Distribution									1Yes	2No	1Yes						1Yes			
Educational																				
Environmental																				
Financial	1Yes								5Yes	3No	4Yes								6Yes	
Health-Related & Social																				
Tourism & Travel-Related									1Yes	1No										
Recreational, Cultural & Sporting																				
Transport	8Yes	3No	1Yes												2Yes		3Yes		1Yes	
Energy			1Yes	2No					2Yes								2Yes			

TABLE 1 (*Cont'd*)

Services	Mexico		NZ		PNG		Peru		Philippines		Russia		Singapore		CT		Thailand		USA		Vietnam	
	ST	MTLT	ST	MTLT	ST	MTLT	ST	MTLT	ST	MTLT	ST	MTLT	ST	MTLT	ST	MTLT	ST	MTLT	ST	MTLT	ST	MTLT
Business													2Yes		1Yes	1						
Communication & Related Engineering													2Yes			2No	4Yes					
Construction																						
Distribution									1Yes													
Educational																						
Environmental																						
Financial															14Yes	1No	1Yes	1No				
Health-Related & Social																						
Tourism & Travel-Related																	1Yes	2No				
Recreational, Cultural & Sporting																						
Transport									1Yes						1Yes		2Yes					
Energy									4Yes													

Total number of short-term commitments achieved (ST Yes): 102
Total number of short-term commitments in process (ST No): 0
Total number of medium/long-term commitments achieved (MT/LT Yes): 0
Total number of medium/long-term commitments in process (MT/LT No): 19

Notes:
Peru, Russia, and Vietnam were not APEC members in 1996.
ST stands for short term, MT stands for medium term, and LT stands for long term.
"Yes" means commitment achieved, and "No" means commitment in the process of implementation.

TABLE 2 **1997 IAP Commitments in Services of APEC Economies**

Services	Australia		Brunei		Canada		Chile		PRC		HK, China		Indonesia		Japan		Korea		Malaysia	
	ST	MTLT	ST	MTLT	ST	MTLT	ST	MTLT	ST	MTLT	ST	MTLT	ST	MTLT	ST	MTLT	ST	MTLT	ST	MTLT
Business	1Yes														1Yes		1Yes			
Communication & Related Engineering													1Yes		8Yes		3Yes	1No		
Construction																	1Yes			
Distribution																				
Educational																				
Environmental																				
Financial	2Yes												1Yes		2Yes					
Health-Related & Social																				
Tourism & Travel-Related																				
Recreational, Cultural & Sporting																				
Transport															1Yes		3Yes			
Energy	1Yes														1Yes		2Yes			

TABLE 2 (*Cont'd*)

Services	Mexico		NZ		PNG		Peru		Philippines		Russia		Singapore		CT		Thailand		USA		Vietnam	
	ST	MTLT	ST	MTLT	ST	MTLT	ST	MTLT	ST	MTLT	ST	MTLT	ST	MTLT	ST	MTLT	ST	MTLT	ST	MTLT	ST	MTLT
Business																						
Communication & Related Engineering													3Yes	1No	1Yes	1No						
Construction																						
Distribution																						
Educational																						
Environmental																						
Financial													5Yes									
Health-Related & Social																						
Tourism & Travel-Related																						
Recreational, Cultural & Sporting																						
Transport															1Yes		1Yes					
Energy																	8Yes					

Total number of short-term commitments achieved (ST Yes): 48
Total number of short-term commitments in process (ST No): 0
Total number of medium/long-term commitments achieved (MT/LT Yes): 0
Total number of medium/long-term commitments in process (MT/LT No): 3

Notes:
Peru, Russia, and Vietnam were not APEC members in 1996.
ST stands for short term, MT stands for medium term, and LT stands for long term.
"Yes" means commitment achieved, and "No" means commitment in the process of implementation.

TABLE 3 **1998 IAP Commitments in Services of APEC Economies**

Services	Australia		Brunei		Canada		Chile		PRC		HK, China		Indonesia		Japan		Korea		Malaysia	
	ST	MTLT	ST	MTLT	ST	MTLT	ST	MTLT	ST	MTLT	ST	MTLT	ST	MTLT	ST	MTLT	ST	MTLT	ST	MTLT
Business	1Yes																1Yes			
Communication & Related				1No	1Yes						2Yes				3Yes		7Yes		1Yes	
Engineering																				
Construction																		1No		
Distribution																				
Educational																				
Environmental									1Yes											
Financial													3Yes	1No	4Yes	1No			2Yes	
Health-Related & Social																				
Tourism & Travel-Related																				
Recreational, Cultural & Sporting																				
Transport	4Yes						1Yes								1Yes		1Yes			
Energy															1Yes	1No		2No		

TABLE 3 (*Cont'd*)

Services	Mexico		NZ		PNG		Peru		Philippines		Russia		Singapore		CT		Thailand		USA		Vietnam	
	ST	MTLT	ST	MTLT	ST	MTLT	ST	MTLT	ST	MTLT	ST	MTLT	ST	MTLT	ST	MTLT	ST	MTLT	ST	MTLT	ST	MTLT
Business																						
Communication & Related Engineering													3Yes	1No	2Yes			1No				
Construction																						
Distribution																						
Educational																						
Environmental																						
Financial															2Yes 2No		1Yes				3Yes	
Health-Related & Social																						
Tourism & Travel-Related																					1Yes	1No
Recreational, Cultural & Sporting																						
Transport																					2Yes	
Energy																						

Total number of short-term commitments achieved (ST Yes): 49
Total number of short-term commitments in process (ST No): 2
Total number of medium/long-term commitments achieved (MT/LT Yes): 0
Total number of medium/long-term commitments in process (MT/LT No): 10

Notes:
ST stands for short term, MT stands for medium term, and LT stands for long term.
"Yes" means commitment achieved, and "No" means commitment in the process of implementation.

TABLE 4 **1999 IAP Commitments in Services of APEC Economies**

Services	Australia		Brunei		Canada		Chile		PRC		HK, China		Indonesia		Japan		Korea		Malaysia	
	ST	MTLT	ST	MTLT	ST	MTLT	ST	MTLT	ST	MTLT	ST	MTLT	ST	MTLT	ST	MTLT	ST	MTLT	ST	MTLT
Business	3Yes																			
Communication & Related Engineering	5Yes										8Yes				4Yes		1Yes		1Yes	
Construction																	1Yes			
Distribution													1Yes							
Educational																				
Environmental																				
Financial	1Yes				2Yes							1No	1Yes		4Yes				7Yes	
Health-Related & Social																				
Tourism & Travel-Related																				
Recreational, Cultural & Sporting																				
Transport	3Yes										1Yes		1Yes		1Yes		1Yes	1No		
Energy															4Yes					

TABLE 4 *(Cont'd)*

Services	Mexico		NZ		PNG		Peru		Philippines		Russia		Singapore		CT		Thailand		USA		Vietnam	
	ST	MTLT	ST	MTLT	ST	MTLT	ST	MTLT	ST	MTLT	ST	MTLT	ST	MTLT	ST	MTLT	ST	MTLT	ST	MTLT	ST	MTLT
Business																					3Yes	
Communication & Related Engineering													1Yes	1No	1Yes		1Yes	1No			4Yes	
Construction																					1Yes	
Distribution																						
Educational																						
Environmental																						
Financial														1No		1No						
Health-Related & Social																						
Tourism & Travel-Related																						
Recreational, Cultural & Sporting																						
Transport															1Yes						1Yes	
Energy																						

Total number of short-term commitments achieved (ST Yes): 63
Total number of short-term commitments in process (ST No): 0
Total number of medium/long-term commitments achieved (MT/LT Yes): 0
Total number of medium/long-term commitments in process (MT/LT No): 6

Notes:
ST stands for short term, MT stands for medium term, and LT stands for long term.
"Yes" means commitment achieved, and "No" means commitment in the process of implementation.

TABLE 5 **Summary of APEC Economies' IAP Commitments in Services**

	1996				1997				1998				1999				Total			
Services	ST Yes	ST No	MTLT Yes	MTLT No	ST Yes	ST No	MTLT Yes	MTLT No	ST Yes	ST No	MTLT Yes	MTLT No	ST Yes	ST No	MTLT Yes	MTLT No	ST Yes	ST No	MTLT Yes	MTLT No
Business	14	0	0	1	3	0	0	0	5	0	0	0	6	0	0	0	28	0	0	1
Communication & Related Engineering	22	0	0	3	16	0	0	3	17	0	0	3	24	2	0	2	79	2	0	11
Construction	1	0	0	0	1	0	0	0	0	0	0	1	2	0	0	0	4	0	0	1
Distribution	4	0	0	2	0	0	0	0	0	0	0	0	1	0	0	0	5	0	0	2
Educational	0	0	0	0	0	0	0	0	0	0	0	0	0	0	0	0	0	0	0	0
Environmental	0	0	0	0	0	0	0	0	1	0	0	0	0	0	0	0	1	0	0	0
Financial	31	0	0	5	10	0	0	0	15	2	0	2	15	0	0	3	71	2	0	10
Health-Related & Social	0	0	0	0	0	0	0	0	0	0	0	0	0	0	0	0	0	0	0	0
Tourism & Travel-Related	2	0	0	3	0	0	0	0	1	0	0	1	0	0	0	0	3	0	0	4
Recreational, Cultural & Sporting	0	0	0	0	0	0	0	0	0	0	0	0	0	0	0	0	0	0	0	0
Transport	19	0	0	3	6	0	0	0	9	0	0	0	9	0	0	1	43	0	0	4
Energy	9	0	0	2	12	0	0	0	1	0	0	3	4	0	0	0	26	0	0	5

Notes:
ST stands for short term, MT stands for medium term, and LT stands for long term.
"Yes" means commitment achieved, and "No" means commitment in the process of implementation.

members have not yet reported commitments in educational services, health-related and social services, and recreation, cultural, and sporting services, even though these categories of services could be included in the IAPs.

There are a few things to note when analysing the tables. First, the higher number of commitments by an economy does not mean that it is becoming more liberalized than others. Some developed economies that already have low barriers to trade in services might have few or no commitments in the IAPs. For example, the United States has stated since the 1996 IAP that it "has one of the most open regimes in the world for trade and investment in services" (APEC 1996). This study has not located any specific U.S. commitments in IAPs.

Additionally, the commitments stated in the IAPs do not share the same degree of specificity and complexity. This means that some commitments are more easily achieved relative to others. For example, a commitment that states that certain laws will be reviewed is easier to accomplish then a commitment that promises to change laws to facilitate trade in services. A review does not necessarily lead to change while a commitment to change laws within a time-frame is more specific and complicated.

In summary, the main purpose of this study is to examine whether or not APEC economies have implemented their commitments in IAPs. The data indicate that members have completed commitments within the deadline. At present, the wording and substance of most of the commitments need to be changed before they can be considered useful in helping members achieve the Bogor objectives of free trade and investment. The necessary changes are discussed in the recommendations.

Recommendations

Recently, the APEC economies have recognized the need to make substantial changes to the reporting format of IAPs. APEC has developed the E-IAP. The purpose is to allow easy access to the IAPs. Concurrently, APEC is also aware of the necessity to streamline the reporting process. Researchers, businessmen, and government officials have considered IAPs to be the main source of information to locate members' commitments to achieve the Bogor objectives. After producing several IAPs, it became apparent that IAPs have not been clear and precise in presenting information on commitments. The reporting format is not always followed, so that a reader would have to spend time sifting through the information.

Australia is taking the lead in standardizing the summary reports of IAPs. The Australian plan is to come up with one simple format to summarize commitments. The title of the new format is "Summary Report on Commitments Achieved and Improvements Planned: IAP for [economy]." The format consists of three columns. The first column states the IAP chapter. The second column indicates new measures implemented, that is, commitments achieved. The plans for further improvements in the future or new commitments are listed in the third column. Australia welcomes APEC economies to use the new format for reporting on commitments. The reasons given are that: 1) the format would simplify the reporting process; 2) it would result in the methodical and comprehensive statement of commitments; and 3) consistency in presentation would lead to reader-friendliness (APEC 2000b).

This study agrees with Australia that the new format is beneficial to everyone interested in understanding members' commitments. In addition, the format's greater clarity of presentation would simplify the monitoring of commitments, that is, whether or not economies have implemented their commitments. It must be stressed that economies need to ensure that all commitments are stated in the summary report, which includes both commitments achieved and new ones. Members have to make sure that when new commitments are listed, they will be stated in the implemented column upon completion. There might be cases where economies list commitments achieved but they were not included in earlier reports under the section on new commitments. When this situation occurs, economies could include a brief note.

Another aspect of IAPs that necessitates improvement is the description of the commitments. In reviewing the commitments in the IAPs, one common problem encountered was the lack of detail in the description. Tang (2000) has stated that the lack of clearly articulated commitments in the IAP is the major impediment to the implementation of IAP commitments. Similarly, Wong (2000) has reported that many IAP commitments are vague, so that specific information, such as action to be followed, market sectors to be liberalized, goals, and deadlines, should be stated. This study recommends that members should provide more information. The commitments should be specific. For example, it is not adequate to state that financial services will be liberalized. As long as one can continue to ask what aspect of financial services will be liberalized, more description is necessary, if that information is available. In the case of completed commitments, the description should clearly state what has been implemented. Furthermore, the commitments should include time-frames for implementation. It would be useful to state whether or not the commitments are the result of WTO negotiations.

In addition, there is the need for greater dialogue among government officials, businesses, and interest groups within an economy, so that commitments to liberalize trade in services could be implemented smoothly and according to schedule. The reason is that there are instances when businesses and interest groups have prevented governments from taking liberalization measures. For example, Kim (2000) has noted that in Korea, businesses and interest groups have opposed liberalization in the motion picture industry, legal services, and medical services. In the case of Hong Kong, stock brokerages have been resisting market liberalization (Wong 2000). The bottom line, however, is the necessary existence of strong governmental support to enhance the implementation process. A government that has the will to implement the IAP commitments would greatly strengthen the implementation process, since the APEC process is based on voluntarism.

References

APEC. "United States' Individual Action Plan". Singapore: APEC Secretariat, 1996. Available at <http://www.apecsec.org.sg/iap/iap.html>.

_____. "Convenor Report: First Meeting of the APEC Group on Services (GOS)". Singapore: APEC Secretariat, 1997a. Available at <http://www.apecsec.org.sg/virtualib/v-gos.html>.

_____. "Convenor's Report: Second Meeting of the APEC Group on Services (GOS)". Singapore: APEC Secretariat, 1997b. Available at <http://www.apecsec.org.sg/virtualib/v-gos.html>.

_____. "Convenor's Summary Record of Discussion for the 11th Meeting of GOS". Singapore: APEC Secretariat, 2000a. Available at <http://www.apecsec.org.sg/virtualib/v-gos.html>.

_____. "Summary Report on IAP Achievements and Future Plans." Letter distributed to APEC Senior Officials by Australia's Ministry of Foreign Affairs and Trade, 2000b.

Feinberg, Richard. "Building the APEC International Assessment Network." Letter distributed at the APEC Study Centre Consortium Conference, Auckland, New Zealand, 31 May – 2 June 1999a.

_____. "List of APEC Issue Areas". List distributed at the APEC Study Centre Consortium Conference, Auckland, New Zealand, 31 May – 2 June 1999b.

_____. "Summary of Workshop Consensus". Memorandum distributed at the APEC Study Centre Consortium Conference, Auckland, New Zealand, 31 May – 2 June 1999c.

Findlay, Christopher, and Tony Warren. "Impediments to Services Sector Trade and Investment." Australian Research Council, 1999. Mimeographed.

Kim, June-Dong. "Responses to APIAN Services' Questionnaire for Korea." APIAN Services' Questionnaire completed by the Korea Institute for International Economic Policy, 2000.

PECC. *Assessing APEC Individual Action Plans and their Contribution to APEC's Goals*. Singapore: PECC International Secretariat, 1999.

Tang, Cheong Meng. "Responses to APIAN Services Questionnaire for Singapore. APIAN Services". Questionnaire completed by the Institute of Southeast Asian Studies, Singapore, 2000.

Wong, Clement. "Responses to APIAN Services Questionnaire for Hong Kong." APIAN Services Questionnaire completed by the City University of Hong Kong, 2000.

Yamazawa, Ippei. *APEC's Progress toward the Bogor Target: A Quantitative Assessment of Individual Action Plans*. Tokyo: Japan National Committee for Pacific Economic Cooperation and APEC Study Centre/Hitotsubashi University, 1997.

Yamazawa, Ippei, and Shujiro Urata. "Trade and Investment Liberalization and Facilitation." Paper prepared for the 25th PAFTAD meeting, Osaka, 16–18 June 1999.

59- 70

3

APEC'S COMMITMENTS ON INVESTMENT

MYRNA S. AUSTRIA

076
019
F14/
F15

Summary of Key Initiatives

The long-term goal of APEC is to achieve free and open trade and investment by 2010 for its developed member economies and by 2020 for its developing member economies. As stated in the Osaka Action Agenda (OAA), a free and open investment environment in the Asia-Pacific region can be achieved through liberalization of investment regimes by progressively providing for most-favoured-nation (MFN) treatment and national treatment, and ensuring transparency; and by facilitating investment activities through technical assistance and cooperation.

To attain the above goal, the OAA has set guidelines for member economies to follow. Economies are to progressively reduce or eliminate exceptions and restrictions using as an initial framework the WTO Agreement, the APEC Non-Binding Investment Principles, any other international agreements relevant to each economy, and any commonly agreed guidelines developed in APEC; as well as to explore the expansion of APEC's network of bilateral investment agreements.

The Leaders have announced, through the annual APEC Economic Leaders' Declaration, a number of broad initiatives that give the general direction on how member economies should advance the liberalization process of investment in the region. Some of these initiatives include the following.

Investment Policy

1. Updating of the *APEC Investment Guidebook on Investment Regimes*;
2. Expansion and acceleration of APEC's trade and investment facilitation programmes to complement and support the liberalization process;
3. Support of trade and investment programmes with appropriate technical assistance to maximize the effectiveness of APEC activities;
4. Consultations on economic growth strategies, regional capital flows, and other macroeconomic issues to facilitate regional investment flows, and strengthen APEC's dialogue on economic policy issues;
5. Strengthening of efforts to improve the collection and sharing of services trade and investment data;
6. Development of a menu of options to enhance the environment for investment that members can voluntarily choose to include in their Individual Action Plans (IAPs);
7. Rapid implementation of measures to further enhance an environment conducive for trade and investment flows through the adoption of the menu of options and measures on investment and the conduct of an FDI (foreign direct investment) mart; and
8. Strengthening of trade and investment flows in the region by working on competition policy and regulatory reforms.

Methodology and Scope of the Report

This chapter tries to evaluate the progress in the implementation of the various initiatives and commitments made by member economies, either individually or collectively, to achieve free and open investment in the region. This study made use of the various reports of the Investment Expert Group (IEG) and the 1999 IAPs. Reference was also made to the results of existing studies. However, owing to time constraints in the preparation of this report, the IAPs of only eight (8) economies, representing different levels of development and geographic locations in the region, were considered in the report. These include Australia, Canada, Chile, Chinese Taipei, People's Republic of China, Philippines, Singapore, and South Korea.

To evaluate the effectiveness of the implementation of commitments to achieve the OAA, questionnaires were circulated to selected experts on investment in each of the APEC member economies. The questionnaire covered three major areas, namely, evaluation of effective progress in the implementation of the initiatives, assessment of the strengths and weaknesses in the implementation of the initiatives, and identification of possible recommendations to strengthen the implementation of the initiatives. However, among the economies, only Chile and South Korea returned the completed questionnaires. Hence, the results of the questionnaire cannot be generalized to be representative of all member economies.

Actions Taken at the International Level

In response to the goals, APEC economies have committed to implement a number of initiatives collectively. These commitments are contained in the Collective Action Plan (CAP) and are guided by the following objectives:

1. Increase, in the short term, the transparency of APEC investment regimes by (i) updating the *APEC Investment Guidebook on Investment Regimes* as appropriate to reflect changes in regimes; (ii) establishing software networks on investment regulations and investment opportunities; and (iii) improving the state of statistical reporting and data collection;
2. Promote, in the short term, an ongoing mechanism for dialogue with the APEC business community on ways to improve the APEC investment environment;
3. Identify, in the short term, ongoing technical cooperation needs in the Asia-Pacific region and organize training programmes which will assist APEC economies in fulfilling APEC investment objectives;
4. Establish, in the short term, a dialogue process with the Organization for Economic Cooperation and Development (OECD) and other international fora involved in global and regional investment issues;
5. Define and implement, in the short term, follow-up training from the Uruguay Round implementation seminars;
6. Undertake an evaluation of the role of investment liberalization in economic development in the Asia-Pacific region;
7. Study, in the medium term, possible common elements between existing subregional arrangements relevant to investment;
8. Refine, in the medium term, APEC's understanding of "free and open investment"; and
9. Assess, in the long term, the merits of developing an APEC-wide discipline on investment in the light of APEC's own progress in the medium term, as well as developments in other international fora.

The Manila Action Plan for APEC (MAPA, 1996) contained the initial commitments of member economies to implement the CAP on

BOX 1
Completed Projects Under the Collective Action Plan On Investment, 1996–2000

A. Transparency

1. Published 3rd and 4th editions of the *APEC Investment Guidebook*;
2. Updated the electronic version of the *APEC Investment Guidebook*; and
3. Compiled the compendium of Initiatives, Development Efforts, Aspiration and Strategies (IDEAS) of the four major stakeholders in foreign direct investment (foreign direct investor, home economy, host economy, and domestic investor)*

B. Policy Dialogue

1. Organized five APEC Investment Symposia;
2. Established policy discussions to review investment regimes of the following countries: Chile, Japan, Papua New Guinea, Malaysia, Chinese Taipei, Australia, Philippines, Mexico, New Zealand, Peru and People's Republic of China*;
3. Established policy dialogues to review the investment aspects of the following Free Trade Areas: Canada-Chile Free Trade Area, the ASEAN Investment Area and the Mexico-Chile Free Trade Area;
4. Developed, in conjunction with the business sector, a menu of options for investment liberalization and business facilitation to strengthen APEC economies which member economies could include in their IAPs*;
5. Updated the menu options to expand and include new options*;
6. Organized the first APEC Investment Mart (Seoul);
7. Conducted the Second Business Survey; and
8. Conducted a study on the impact of investment liberalization; and briefing on the results of the study*

C. Economic and Technical Cooperation

1. Conducted.training programmes and seminars for officials concerned with investment in the following areas:
   - Implementation of the Uruguay Round Trade Related Investment Measures (TRIMs) agreement;
   - Experiences of APEC economies with one-stop investment agencies;
   - FDI Policy and Administration Adjustment; and
   - Start-up companies and venture capital
   - Strategies to identify and facilitate investment in specific areas, for example, SMEs, development and industrial linkage, high tech industries, and R&D activities;
   - Workshops (3) for APEC investment/trade officials to understand and be informed of the various options for investment liberalization and business facilitation; and
   - Improving member economies' capabilities on statistical reporting and data collection.

Notes:
1. Projects with asterisk (*) were not included in the original 1996 OAA Collective Actions.
2. APEC also implements projects and activities on a continuing basis but they are not included in this list.

SOURCE: Convenor's Summary Report on Investment (various years).

investment. Since then, the CAP has been updated annually. Box 1 shows a summary of completed projects implemented for the period 1996–2000. In general, significant progress has been made in the implementation of the collective actions. The projects represent a balanced package of investment liberalization, facilitation, and technical cooperation. They are also consistent with the broad initiatives outlined by the Leaders in their annual declarations. Most noteworthy, however, is the fact that efforts under the CAP have been expanded by including projects that were not originally included in the OAA collective action. In other words, these are "additions or improvements" to the original OAA.

The projects covered three major areas, namely, transparency, policy dialogue, and economic and technical cooperation. In the area of *transparency*, the aims of the projects were to (i) enhance transparency in investment regimes; (ii) promote easy access by the business sector to authoritative investment-related information; and (iii) create greater awareness among government officials involved in multilateral negotiations on the interests and concerns of the four stakeholders of foreign direct investment (foreign investor, home economy, host economy, and domestic investor). The most notable achievement in promoting transparency is the publication of the *APEC Investment Guidebook*. The *Guidebook*, which is available in both hard copy and electronic format on the Internet for easy access by the business community, has been updated to reflect changes in the economies' investment regimes. The *Guidebook* is now in its fourth edition.

On the other hand, *policy dialogues* were undertaken as (i) a strategy for information exchange between business and government on investment issues to enhance the investment environment and promote investment flows in the region; and as (ii) a venue for informing potential investors of member economies on the investment opportunities available within APEC, and for seeking views from the business sector about priorities for APEC's investment liberalization. The dialogues have been facilitated by an annual investment symposium since 1996, and beginning in 2000, an annual investment mart.

The most outstanding accomplishment so far in promoting policy dialogues is the development of the Menu of Options. The Menu is a list of policy measures from which member economies may voluntarily select a number of options for inclusion in their IAPs in order to advance towards creating a free and open investment regime. The list includes policy measures on investment in general and on specific areas, such as transparency, non-discrimination, expropriation and compensation, protection from strife and similar events, transfer of capital related to investments, performance requirements, entry and stay of personnel, settlement of disputes, intellectual property, avoidance of double taxation, and facilitating measures to improve the business environment. Since its development in 1999, the Menu has been updated to include other policy areas, such as technology transfer.

Under *economic and technical cooperation*, activities include seminars and training aimed at improving the knowledge of APEC investment officials on enhancing their investment environment.

While there was considerable progress in the implementation of the collective actions, the projects implemented since 1996 have covered only those that addressed short-term objectives. Efforts have yet to start in identifying and implementing projects covering objectives (7), (8) and (9) of the OAA collective actions, as outlined above. These areas cover medium- to long-term objectives. Efforts should therefore be directed towards this end, together with the inclusion of clear time-frames for the implementation of these collective actions.

Furthermore, the implementation of the projects is just the first step towards the Bogor goal. How far these projects have contributed towards achieving the Bogor goal of free and open investment is yet to be evaluated. The next step therefore should be an assessment of the impact of these collective actions.

Actions Taken at the Individual Economy Level

Liberalization of Investment Regimes

The PECC (1999) study developed an indicator system to measure the openness of investment policy based on the 1996 *APEC Investment Guidebook*. Changes in investment policy were measured by updating this indicator system using policy changes documented in the IAPs for each economy between 1996 and 1998. The study shows that "there are now far fewer economies in APEC which can be defined as having relatively closed investment regimes" (PECC 1999, p.54). The most significant change in policy occurred in the areas of market access, approval procedures, and facilitation. The investment liberalization made by the member economies has been consistent with the WTO rules. In many cases, members have gone beyond the WTO framework since the WTO-TRIMs (trade-related investment measures) deal only with those related to trade, such as local content requirements, but not those more fundamental to FDI, such as market access.

The same study shows that in terms of the level of development, developing member economies have made considerable commitments to FDI liberalization. Hence, the gap in the level of openness in FDI regimes among the member economies has narrowed between 1996 and 1998.

Progress in the Implementation of APEC Non-Binding Investment Principles

Principles

Table 1 shows the degree of compliance by member economies with the APEC Non-Binding Investment Principles (NBIP) based on an assessment of the 1999 IAPs. The APEC NBIP are principles for strengthening the efficiency of investment administration, eliminating investment obstacles, and establishing a free and open investment environment in the region. They are non-binding in nature and absent of customary provisions that specify procedures with respect to exceptions and reservations.

As shown in the table, none of the eight economies evaluated has complied with *all* the twelve principles. Nonetheless, most of them are complying with almost all the principles. Most of the economies still have restrictions or reservations on the principles on national treatment, performance requirements, and entry and sojourn of personnel. Nonetheless, for some of these economies, where there are restrictions or exceptions in their current commitments, actions in the short to medium and long term have been identified. Likewise, where restrictions/exceptions are temporary, a definite timetable that matches the WTO deadline is indicated.

Some economies have gone beyond the requirements of some of the principles. For example, the principle on the removal of barriers to capital exports requires that economies minimize the regulatory and institutional barriers to the outflow of investment. Some of the economies (like Australia) have totally removed the barriers. Moreover, on the principle of national treatment, China extends more preferential treatment to foreign enterprises than to domestic enterprises in certain policy areas, such as tax policy, and import and export rights.

Expansion of APEC's Network of Bilateral Investment Agreements

Based on the evaluation of the 1999 IAPs, most of the economies are progressively increasing their bilateral investment agreements not only with other APEC economies but also with non-APEC countries. For example, Chinese Taipei has signed agreements with 25 countries, 5 of which are APEC members; the Philippines has signed with 26 countries, 8 of which are APEC members; Singapore has signed with 27 countries; and South Korea has 59 bilateral investment agreements. These agreements cover reciprocal protection and non-discrimination of investment, free transfer of capital, payments and earnings, freedom from expropriation and nationalization, recognition of the principle of subrogation, among others. Some of the economies have also acceded to the Multilateral Investment Agreements. Some APEC economies are also members of free trade areas — such as the North America Free Trade Agreement (NAFTA), the ASEAN Free Trade Area (AFTA), and the Canada-Chile Free Trade Area — where investment is a significant area for liberalization.

Investment Facilitation

Based on the 1999 IAPs, all the economies have reported strategies/ activities that would attract, expand, and facilitate the flow of investment into their economies. Among others, these include a one-stop action centre, an investment promotion network, foreign trade service corps, and the appointment of a strategic investment coordinator.

Evaluation of Effective Progress

A questionnaire was used to evaluate how far the implementation of the CAP and the non-binding investment principles have advanced towards the APEC goal of free and open investment in the region. Experts were asked to rate each of the areas as either poor, modest, good, or excellent. As indicated earlier, only two economies completed the questionnaire.

The effectiveness of the implementation of the initiatives differs with each economy. The effectiveness of the non-binding investment principles in one economy was evaluated as excellent in all but one principle (namely, investment incentives, which was evaluated as good) (see Table 1 for the list of principles). In the other economy, however, seven of the principles were rated as good in their effectiveness, and the rest (five) were rated as modest.

On the CAP of one economy, the effectiveness of six of the nine objectives (as outlined earlier) was evaluated as good in terms of how far they have advanced towards the OAA, while three were evaluated as excellent. In the other economy, however, only one objective was evaluated as excellent; the others were rated as good (2 areas), modest (5 areas) and poor (1 area). The area that was rated as poor addresses a long-term objective; and this is consistent with the findings mentioned earlier that efforts have not been directed towards implementing the medium- to long-term collective actions.

Experts were also asked whether the current commitments in the IAPs and CAP are adequate for APEC to advance towards its goal of a free and open investment environment. The results show that the current IAPs and CAP are considered as not adequate for the economies to advance towards the APEC goal, as additional impediments to foreign investment exist. In order to attain a genuinely free and open investment,

TABLE 1 **Progress in the Implementation of the APEC Non-Binding Investment Principles**

Principles	Australia	Canada	China	Chinese Taipei	Chile	Philippines	South Korea	Singapore
Transparency	—	—	—			—	—	—
Non-discrimination between Sources	—	—	—		With minor exceptions	—	—	
National Treatment	With limited restrictions	— —	With restrictions	With restrictions under negative list	With minor exceptions	With restrictions under negative list	With restrictions under negative list	With limited restrictions
Investment Incentives	—		—			—		—
Performance Requirements	With limited use	With limited reservation in certan areas			With minor exceptions	Temporary exception with definite timetable		—
Expropriation and Compensation	—	—	—			—		—
Repatriation and Convertibility	—	—	Subject to existing laws		Subject to existing laws	—	—	—
Settlement of Disputes	—	—	—		Subject to existing laws	—		—
Entry and Sojourn of Personnel	Subect to existing laws		—	Subject to existing laws	With minor exceptions	Subject to existing laws		—
Avoidance of Double Taxation	—					—	—	—
Investor Behaviour	—							—
Removal of Barriers to Capital Exports	—					Subject to administrative regulations		—

Notes: 1. A check mark (—) stands for compliance with the principle;
2. No entry implies absence of information on the subject in the IAP.

SOURCE: 1999 IAPs

the economies need to identify and make an inventory of the various kinds of investment impediments and endeavour to remove them. The business community is expecting more liberal proposals and a deeper commitment from the economies to work towards the attainment of the goal.

The experts have noted, however, that their economies have implemented other initiatives that have contributed to the furtherance of attaining a free and open investment regime but which were not included in their commitments in the IAPs. This includes the liberalization of certain sectors and the negotiations of bilateral investment agreements. One expert concluded that the investment regime of his economy was more open than that expressed in the IAP.

Assessment of Strengths and Weaknesses

Experts were also asked to identify the factors that they considered to have contributed to the success of the implementation of their economy's commitments in investment. The most important factors identified were strong government support, and that the commitments were part of the economies' unilateral liberalization efforts.

The other factors, ranked in order of importance, are: (1) similar commitments made in other fora like the WTO, AFTA, and NAFTA; (2) adequate finance for the implementation; (3) strong civil society participation; (4) strong private/business participation; and (5) peer pressure from other APEC economies.

On the other hand, the factors that were regarded to have hindered or led to the slow or non-implementation of the commitments include the following, ranked in order of importance: (1) opposition from private/business sector; (2) opposition from civil society; and (3) inadequate funding support.

Conclusion and Recommendations

Significant progress has been made in implementing the collective actions aimed at achieving the Bogor goal of free and open investment in the region. Most of the economies included in the study have also complied with almost all of the non-binding investment principles, thereby improving their investment regimes. Other initiatives have also been implemented as additions or improvements, both to the original OAA and the individual commitments of member economies in their IAPs.

Nonetheless, most of the accomplishments thus far, while representing a balanced package of investment liberalization, facilitation and economic and technical cooperation, address only the short-term objectives spelled out in the OAA, leaving the medium to long-term objectives untouched.

At best, the current collective and individual actions focused only on improving the investment environment and are not sufficient to assure the attainment of the Bogor goals as additional impediments to foreign investment exist.

Several issues need to be addressed by APEC to keep it on track towards its 2010/2020 deadline. First, actions and projects that address the medium to long-term objectives of the OAA should now be identified with a clear timetable and benchmarks so as to aid monitoring and assessment. These objectives include (i) the refinement of APEC's understanding of "free and open investment"; and (ii) an assessment of the merits of developing an APEC-wide discipline on investment. To this day, APEC is still unclear on what exactly is free and open investment.

Secondly, there needs to be coordinated action on investment incentives. The current competition in terms of augmenting incentives to attract more investment runs the risk of being a negative-sum game, which just transfers national wealth to foreign investors. In order to prevent this harmful competition, member economies should focus on rules-based competition, not on incentives-based competition.

Thirdly, there is a need to accelerate investment liberalization so that the economies will not face considerable adjustment problems as they approach the deadline of free and open investment. One strategy for doing this is to include a complete inventory on investment impediments in the IAPs. This will provide useful information to potential investors and will serve as a means of exerting pressure on the economies to accelerate liberalization. Furthermore, almost all economies still have restrictions in implementing the principle on national treatment. This has become an important barrier to foreign investment.

Finally, more work on evaluating the impact of investment liberalization should be done. A clear understanding of the impacts of investment liberalization and the dissemination of these to the public would lessen resistance to further liberalization.

References

APEC. *1999 Individual Action Plans* (1999). Available at <http://www.apecsec.org.sg>

_____. *Review of CAP Implementation since 1996*. Available at <http://www.apecsec.org.sg>

_____. *Convenor's Summary Report on Investment*, various years. Available at <http://www.apecsec.org.sg>

———. *APEC Economic Leaders' Declaration*, various years. Available at <http://www.apecsec.org.sg>

———. *APEC Ministerial Meeting Joint Statement*, various years. Available at <http://www.apecsec.org.sg>

———. *Manila Action Plan for APEC*, Volume I, 1996.

APEC Secretariat. *Selected APEC Documents*. Singapore, 1995.

PECC. *Assessing APEC Individual Action Plans and their Contribution to APEC's Goals*. Manila, 1999.

4

COMPETITION POLICY AND REGULATORY REFORM

MERIT E. JANOW

Summary of the Issue

In support of the Bogor goals of free and open trade and investment by 2010/2020, APEC has promoted activities that will strengthen the operation of markets and improve the role of competition (major themes promoted by the 1999 APEC Chair). A dimension of this effort is aimed at developing a shared understanding of competition policy issues among APEC economies. More specifically, in 1994, the APEC Ministers agreed that the Committee on Trade and Investment would develop an understanding of competition issues, notably the laws and policies of economies in the region. In 1996, the Osaka Action Agenda work programmes for competition policy and economic deregulation were combined. More recently, at the APEC Summit in September 1999, the Leader's Declaration supported "growth through strong and open markets", including by "enhancing the role of competition to improve efficiency and broaden participation by enterprises". The Declaration also "endorsed the APEC Principles to Enhance Competition and Regulatory Reform". The Declaration stated that the principles "provide a core part of the framework for strengthening our markets which will better integrate individual and collective actions by APEC economies to achieve those goals".

With respect to competition policy, each APEC economy has undertaken to review its competition policy and/or laws; implement as appropriate technical assistance in regard to policy development, legislative drafting and the powers and functions of enforcement agencies; and establish appropriate cooperation arrangements among APEC economies. This Issue Report considers actions taken by member economies and expert assessments of the APEC Principles.

Actions taken at the International Level

None of the respondents commented in detail on the actions taken at the international level, although several respondents noted the annual APEC seminar on competition policy.[1]

Actions taken by Member Economies[2]

Several of the respondents identified a number of measures that had been taken within their own jurisdiction to further the APEC undertakings on competition and economic deregulation. These are summarized in brief below.

Philippines: Evaluation of the 1998 and 1999 stated measures that would be undertaken by the government.

Through a variety of measures, the Philippine Government was identified as accepting the need for a competition policy framework that should go hand in hand with trade liberalization, economic deregulation, and privatization measures. Specific mention was made of measures undertaken to liberalize parts of the services sector, economic deregulation in public utilities, reduction of tariffs and limitations on foreign investment in a number of sectors of the economy, tax reforms, and other measures. Specifically in the area of competition policy, the Philippine Government committed in the 1996 APEC Summit to introduce anti-monopoly laws and policies. The last year has produced a variety of bills that are aimed at promoting competition in the market. President Estrada renewed the government's commitment to pass legislation and establish a Fair Trade Commission. Furthermore, other steps have been taken, including entering into a technical assistance agreement/project with Australia in 1997. Seminars and other deliberations with Australian and other technical experts continued in 1999–2000.

A number of problems particular to the Philippines were also identified. These included the observation that the laws and regulations that have bearing on competition are numerous and varied. These laws have proven inadequate or ineffective in many instances in staving off the ill-effects of anti-competitive structures and behaviour in the market. Competition has not been established economy-wide, nor has existing competition in other sectors of the market-place been enhanced. The reasons include the following: there are a large number of enforcement agencies; there is a conspicuous absence of a comprehensive policy framework in place; there is a lack of clear jurisprudence on competition; some of the laws are penal and the evidentiary requirements are so great that they do not serve as a deterrent. There is also a serious lack of expertise in understanding or implementing competition laws, which rely heavily on economic analysis.

South Korea: Evaluation of the 1998 and 1999 stated measures that would be undertaken by the government.

The 1998 IAP was reported to have been duly implemented in 1999. The Omnibus Cartel Repeal Act and the Fair Trade Labelling and Advertising Act were enacted to abolish or reform some twenty cartels that had been under the protection of about eighteen individual laws, and to restrict unfair or deceptive labelling and advertising activities that may impair reasonable consumer choices. The Fair Trade Commission (FTC) conducted investigations of anti-competitive intra-group transactions, especially concerning cross subsidization. Actions by the Korean Fair Trade Commission (KFTC) have helped to discipline not only anti-competitive behaviour of *chaebol* firms but also cross-subsidization between competitive and non-competitive activities in public corporations such as KPECO. Furthermore, although not mentioned in the 1999 IAP, the development of new M&A (mergers and acquisitions) guidelines was initiated. In the new guidelines, exemption criteria are clearly based on efficiency claims, and the procedures utilized by the competition agency for reviewing transactions were simplified.

Certain amendments to the law have also been introduced that have increased its flexibility in dealing with dominance issues by removing simple structural rules from the statutory definition and eliminating the annual listing of dominant firms. The 1999 amendments to the Fair Trade Act also make it applicable to all sectors of the economy. Previously, some twelve sectors including mining, finance, and seed industries were excluded.

Indonesia: Evaluation of the 1999 stated measures that would be undertaken by the government.

Indonesia has taken a number of legislative and policy steps to promote competition and competition policy in the domestic market. In March

1999, Indonesia promulgated a comprehensive competition law on the Prohibition of Monopolistic Practices and Unfair Business Competition. The law became effective one year thereafter. On 7 June 2000, President Abdurrahman Wahid established the Business Competition Commission, comprised of eleven members. Press reports indicate that the Commission has already suggested that it would investigate possible monopolistic practices in several areas. Establishing the Commission and identifying its members are important first steps. It faces many challenges in addressing practices occurring in the public and private sectors. Indonesia has indicated its intention to further liberalize and decartelize a number of areas in its economy. The year ahead will be an important period of consolidation and implementation of steps initiated. A number of experts from Germany, Canada, Australia, the United States, and Japan have conducted seminars and other technical assistance efforts directed at supporting the efforts of Indonesia's new competition agency.

Evaluation of Progress

None of the respondents elected to offer quantitative evaluations of progress. A number of respondents offered thoughtful commentary on the principles and whether and how they supported APEC-wide objectives. These are detailed below.

Strengths and Weaknesses

Respondents identified the following strengths of the APEC Principles:

1. The strength of the APEC approach is that it can accommodate the diversity of its membership while providing a forum for the promotion of understanding of best practices and convergence over time. It is difficult to see how APEC could proceed otherwise.
2. As a related observation, for developing economies, non-binding principles provide an opportunity for each country to act voluntarily and to take into account the diverse circumstances and different priorities in each of their respective economies.
3. While the Principles are quite limited in terms of indicating or providing a degree of substantive convergence, they nevertheless provide an important framework in which to promote best practices and soft convergence over time. The Principles do go beyond the World Trade Organization (WTO) and the Organization for Economic Cooperation and Development (OECD) work under way and therefore also remain an important input into further international and extra-APEC regional discussions of trade and competition issues.

4. The notion of developing a database of member economy practices and approaches is a useful instrument to promote transparency and further rule making.
5. The Principles have served a useful purpose in bringing APEC into the discussion of trade and competition policy, which is also occurring elsewhere around the world.
6. An important element of the APEC framework is the development of core principles and rules on domestic competition law and its enforcement. Attention is now appropriately focused on those aspects of competition policy which are more relevant for a regional trading system, while also recognizing the development dimension and differences in domestic legal and institutional frameworks.

The identified weaknesses and limitations were:

1. One respondent suggested that the Principles are not, in fact, competition principles but rather free market advocacy principles. They urge reliance on markets, not government or law, except where absolutely necessary to cure market failure or to serve a clearly defined non-economic goal; and they advocate market reliance in an open and non-discriminatory way. Some Principles — for example, transparency, accountability, non-discrimination — are all good governance/ democracy principles. While this notion of market reliance is a good rule of thumb, the specific forms of economic regulation are nation-specific. Hence, there may be a value in developing a subset of like-Asian Pacific economies that can be targeted or grouped in view of their common special needs. In addition, expanded technical assistance could be useful. However, it is unlikely (and unlikely to be helpful) to advocate an extreme form of free market.
2. The measures taken by APEC members in the name of competition principles are so diverse that it is very difficult to generalize or assess such measures under a single approach or methodology. Hence, it is extremely important to develop some benchmarks over time to see if policies and approaches are converging. Some practices, such as approaches to hardcore cartels, may be appropriate subjects for developing more substantive non-binding principles to get over this hurdle.
3. The relationship between APEC's work in this area and that of the OECD and the WTO has not been fully established. Several respondents saw this as a limitation, while other respondents said that it was not clear whether it was really a limitation or weakness of APEC, given

that those organizations had not paid much attention to APEC or the work under way by all of its member economies.

4. The Principles are useful in that they identify broad concepts such as non-discrimination, transparency, and the like. At the same time, these broad notions may not be adequate for assessing whether practices are anti-competitive.
5. While the New Zealand summit provided new visibility and prominence to the theme of competition, it is not clear whether or not this will translate into meaningful reforms within member economies.

General Recommendations

1. Peer review is necessary and important.
2. APEC should consider seeking more business engagement on the question of competition policy, and developing a business outreach plan.
3. APEC should promote greater collaboration with other international and intergovernmental organizations in this issue area.
4. The development of an APEC database on country approaches to competition policies and economic deregulation measures should include a variety of other related information. Investigation strategies, procedural techniques, and evaluation of what comprises the established best practices of competition authorities, from both developed and developing economies, should be compiled and analysed. This would help jurisdictions adapt and incorporate those best practices into their competition regimes so as to avoid mistakes and even courting challenges in the future. The development of a database is very useful. However, it should not be biased in favour of one approach over another.
5. Another related observation is that APEC should develop a more detailed database of alternative competition policy approaches to an identified set of problems. In this way, APEC member economies can better understand what is meant by the term "best practices" as it applies to this issue area. For example, the United States and the European Union are identified as having somewhat divergent approaches to competition problems stemming from market dominance, while approaches to hardcore cartels are more similar. APEC could usefully identify a range of approaches and also those taken by individual member economies on that spectrum.
6. An effective competition law and policy framework requires an institutional design that insulates the competition agency from

political intervention. The establishment of a Fair Trade Commission as an independent, quasi-judicial organization is therefore an essential step towards curbing the abuse of market power and fostering a more competitive market.

7. The mission of a competition agency should be clearly articulated. Some respondents feel that a key purpose is to encourage competitive rivalry between domestic firms in the home market. Some caution that this should not be interpreted as unlimited access to a market by foreign multinationals, since domestic industries are also important.
8. As APEC economies design economic policies, protection from international competitive pressures may be necessary to encourage domestic industries but such protection should be limited to a period of time. Those firms that prove that they cannot make the necessary adjustments should not be permitted to survive indefinitely.
9. It is important to have an advocate for competition in the formulation of government policies. Information dissemination is an important component as it fosters better understanding and popular support for competition policy to the benefit of business, government, and consumers.
10. Developed economies should provide additional technical assistance in competition policies to developing economies. Moreover, there may be some value in additional collaboration between international organizations that are concerned about competition policy matters (such as the WTO, OECD, UNCTAD, and World Bank) and directing that collaboration towards the concerns and interests of APEC economies.
11. IAP assessments in this policy area should be phased over several years, not undertaken on an annual basis. The reason is that reform measures can take several years to get under way and are often difficult to evaluate, especially just after their introduction.
12. Instead of focusing on the entire gamut of regulatory or competition reforms, the APEC review process should focus on liberalization/competition issues that affect international trade.
13. Additional scholarly efforts should be undertaken to analyse and better explain the relationship between competition policy and economic growth and performance; the impact of regulatory reform measures already undertaken in the region; and elements behind successes and failures. Such in-depth studies are needed to inform policy-making and contribute to achieving the goals of the Bogor Declaration.

Notes

1. The Issue Coordinator is aware that there has been a variety of APEC symposia undertaken on competition policy — for example, in Brunei and elsewhere — which have not been reflected in expert responses to the questionnaire. Furthermore, a considerable degree of preparatory work was undertaken in developing the Principles, based in part on outreach and analysis by independent experts of the existing competition laws and policies in the region. This database is itself part of the foundation that continues to inform APEC deliberations. Certainly, some officials from the APEC economies that are participating in APEC activities on competition policy are also active participants of comparable activities in the OECD, the WTO Working Group, and elsewhere.
2. Regrettably, only a few respondents chose to summarize the actions taken at the level of member economies while a larger set of respondents addressed strengths and weaknesses of the Principles and offered recommendations for appropriate next steps.

5

MOBILITY OF BUSINESS PEOPLE IN APEC

LEONARDO A. LANZONA

Summary of Key Initiatives

In 1996, the APEC Business Advisory Council (ABAC) called on the Economic Leaders to examine closely cross-border flows, particularly of "impediments to flows of people, goods, services, information and capital across borders" that would have a direct effect on business. Such a call was aimed at building a "more productive 'borderless' regional business community." Business mobility — the flow of people across borders — is a major part of this vision and wholly consistent with the view that globalization of trade and capital will inevitably lead to a globalization of movement of people, without relinquishing the control of the state over borders and immigration processes.

Even before 1996, the Osaka Action Agenda of November 1995 actually invited APEC members to improve business mobility by exchanging information on regulatory regimes, streamlining the processing of short-term business visitor visas and procedures for temporary residence of business people, and maintaining a dialogue on these issues with the business community.

The APEC Business Travel Card (ABTC) system was then launched in 1997 with an initial trial. Since that time, eight economies have joined the travel card scheme, with Australia as convenor. The interest in expanding the scope and coverage of the ABTC scheme to more APEC member economies has been on the agenda of ABAC ever since through its Business Facilitation Task Force and the Committee on Trade and Investments. While it will necessarily have to be expanded economy by economy, there is more than some interest on the part of the business sector to enhance business mobility within a reasonably short time horizon as the region emerges from the financial crisis of 1997.

The ABTC scheme, now incorporated in the Individual Action Plans (IAPs) of APEC, consists of two main objectives:

- *Temporary business entry*: The temporary entry of foreign business people to enable them to come to APEC member economies for periods of up to four years to conduct legitimate business and business-related employment that will benefit the individual economies; and
- *Business migration*: The accessibility of business people to permanent residency in APEC economies as long as they meet certain requirements, such as the possession of skills to establish and manage a business in a competitive climate as members of a business; or are senior executives or investors who have actually managed a portfolio and are now looking to relocate to another APEC economy and start a business.

With business travel as one of its priorities, ABAC has formulated recommendations that have guided the agenda on business mobility, resulting in the formation of an Informal Experts Group on Business Mobility (IEGBM) that will inform ABAC of its progress. Business has been closely consulted in the development of the APEC Business Travel Card scheme. The IEGBM Chair recently met with the ABAC Business Facilitation working group at the February 2000 ABAC meeting in Bangkok, Thailand, and ABAC has been invited to attend all IEGBM meetings.

Moreover, even as cooperation in immigration and technical assistance among APEC economies has to date been largely *ad hoc* and based on bilateral arrangements, the project on Business Mobility is expected to address these concerns through coordinated immigration training and the provision of technical assistance to a wide range of APEC economies on a multilateral basis that is directed by the Business Mobility Group. Border control agencies will not only benefit from this coordinated training programme but they will also be able to establish important networks leading to further cooperation and assistance in document fraud control and streamlining entry arrangements. These assistance programmes will also enable economies to develop further business entry arrangements outlined in the Collective Action Plan of the Experts Group on Business Mobility, including improved visa-waiver arrangements, participation in the APEC Business Travel Card scheme, and expanded use of multiple-entry visas for business travellers.

Collective Initiatives

All APEC members have committed to the following:

- To agree in principle to adopt improved service standards for processing applications for, and extensions of, temporary residence permits for executives, managers, and specialists transferred within their companies to other APEC economies.
- To issue multiple-entry visas to frequent business travellers from other APEC economies. They have acted individually to facilitate business travel, for example, by expanding visa-waiver programmes or extending the validity of multiple-entry visas.
- To launch a technical cooperation programme to help members implement advanced border management techniques.
- To maintain up-to-date information on their requirements for short-term business visas and temporary business residency permits in the Internet version of the *APEC Business Travel Handbook*. The *Handbook* also includes contact information on offices that issue visas across the APEC region.

Australia, Chile, Hong Kong, China, Korea, and the Philippines were the first countries to implement a trial of the APEC Business Travel Card scheme, which offered accredited business travellers visa-free travel and expedited airport processing when visiting participating economies. Malaysia and New Zealand joined the Business Travel Card scheme in 1999, while Thailand joined in February 2000.

The creation of the APEC Business Travel Card was nonetheless deemed as the main mechanism to expedite the relatively freer movement of business people in the region following successful in-country and bilateral models already in place. Initiated by the Council in Manila in November 1996, the ABTC (then reinforced by the APEC Business Visa system) was intended to provide quick processing through immigration lanes in participating economies.

Members have also started to implement agreements to streamline the processing of temporary business residency permits. Technical cooperation in 1999 focused on raising members' capacity to detect document fraud as a means to streamline entry for legitimate business travellers, and a number of training sessions were undertaken in this regard by Australia, Canada, Hong Kong, China, and the United States. Economies participating in these and other sessions included Brunei Darussalam, China, Chile, Indonesia, Korea, Malaysia, Mexico, Papua New Guinea, Peru, the Philippines, Russia, Singapore, Chinese Taipei, and Vietnam.

Actions at the Country Level

In 2000, however, there were only eight members participating in the ABTC scheme, namely, Australia, Malaysia, New Zealand, Korea, Hong Kong, Chile, the Philippines, and Thailand. The Chair of ABAC had reported to the Senior Officials Meeting (SOM) the aim that there be twelve member economies in the card scheme by the end of 2000. In the view of ABAC, the ABTC cannot be considered optimally implemented until all twenty-one countries are participating, and there are no restrictions in individual economies on the number of participants allowed to receive cards.

There are a number of practical as well as security problems, identified by the Department of Immigration and Multicultural Affairs of Australia in February 2000, that will discourage new economies from participating. First, there is a need to streamline procedures for data exchange and card re-issue for new economies joining the ABTC scheme. Previously, the process was work intensive for all economies, and for Australia in particular. The participating economies will need to provide electronically all pre-existing historical data to each economy joining the scheme.

Secondly, there are a number of disagreements over the duration of the ABTC and the underlying provisions. While there has been agreement that the cards should be valid for three years from the date of the most recent pre-clearance, the APEC Card Application System has not been enhanced by Australia to reflect this agreement because of competing projects being given higher priority in the lead-up to the Year 2000 rollover.

Thirdly, although the ABTC Operating Framework (para 3.7) states that the visas or entry authority issued by participating economies for card holders should, where possible, have at least the same validity as that of the card (three years), there are several reasons why the validity of permissions will not match the validity of the card. This may happen because an economy's legislative framework provide only a three-year permission. Time lapses may also occur between the pre-clearance of an application and the issue of the ABTC. While cards will be re-issued when new economies join the scheme, the pre-clearance process will not be repeated by all economies, and permissions will not be extended.

Finally, participating economies will need to individually consider the circumstances under which, or the period after which cardholders should be asked to reapply or resubmit their details in full to the home economy. Economies usually vet ABTC applicants before providing their details to other participating economies. Cardholders need to continue to meet their home economy's eligibility requirements before being pre-cleared by a new economy joining the scheme. Australia believes that each economy can best determine how to manage this process. As a minimum, a criminal conviction check should be required if such a check has not been conducted within the previous three years.

Issues pertinent to the concept continue to be addressed today even as the eight economies continually refine the programme to respond to the basic problems faced by the participating countries. The concerns voiced by all member economies of APEC include sovereignty issues, containment of the number of cards issued based on an accreditation system linked to qualification and selection, and alignment with proper immigration standards.

Benigno N. Ricafort, President of the Philippine Network for SME Foundation, Inc, and a member of the Philippine ABAC, noted, for example, that it took the Philippines some two to three years upon the signing of its participation in 1996 to implement the scheme owing to so-called "logistics differences". Sustaining the programme, however, can be a more serious problem since Philippine cardholders have not found it useful to renew the card after one year, the end of its validity period. Hindrances in terms of protocol are often cited as the cause of this lack of interest since each economy requires different types of regulations.

The same can be said for the rest of the other participating countries. Hidehiro Okayama (2000), Staffer to Mr. Thomas Y. Arai, ABAC Japan, Japan Chamber of Commerce & Industry, noted that Australia has issued some 2,400 cards since the inception of the scheme in 1997, but currently only half of this number (approximately 1,200) are in circulation and in active use by Australian business people.

Nattaporn Boonprapa, Foreign Affairs Officer of the Thai APEC Study Centre, suggested that the full implementation of the ABTC in Thailand may have been hindered by much confusion about its guidelines. At present, various modifications in the application procedures are being proposed so that the programme can be fully enforced by the end of 2000.

Evaluation of the Progress

An improved capacity by APEC economies to detect travel document fraud flowing from a coordinated training and technical assistance programme should lead to the introduction of streamlined entry arrangements for APEC business people. This will reduce the time and effort business people spend obtaining visas and in immigration queues at airports, freeing time for productive business pursuits.

"Lead" economies with sophisticated technical capacity in travel document fraud detection have already been identified and have been asked to help other member economies. This includes Australia/New Zealand, USA, Canada, Japan, and Hong Kong. These lead economies have been providing training and technical assistance to the other economies that have requested assistance in this area. Activities will, in the coming years, comprise evaluation of current processing systems, practices, techniques and training, needs analysis, further travel document fraud training, and step-by-step analysis of necessary improvements for border agency staff in each participant economy.

However, despite this willingness towards streamlining procedures, other APEC countries have not been enthusiastic about joining the programme. What seems to be a main hindrance is the lack of interest on the part of the other APEC economies, especially the more developed countries. Boonprapa noted that to generate attention, it is necessary for the other countries to join the scheme. Because some countries seemingly would not consider participating in the future, he observed that the other APEC members have resorted to other alternative visa facilitation programmes, such as multiple-entry visas and grants for longer stays.

Concerns about security have also been noted as a disincentive since some economies seem eager to see improvements in the security features of the card before participating. A re-design of the card is being proposed to address these security concerns. However, in response to the questionnaire we sent, the APEC Secretariat alludes that the main obstacle for the other countries seems to be the general feeling that the scheme may have adverse effects on employment, hence detrimental to their economies' progress. Ricafort also notes that there exists some preference to accept certain groups of people, but to disallow entry to some sectors, especially the small and medium-scale enterprises.

This lack of enthusiasm from the other countries and the seeming preference for certain forms of mobility can be seen in the presence of varied migration and travel regulations in APEC, as shown in Table 1. Three points are important from this table. First, a number of the economies, primarily members of the Association of the Southeast Asian

Nations (ASEAN), have already established visa-free entry conditions for short-term business travellers. This means that greater openness on the part of these economies to the notion of business mobility is needed. Chile and New Zealand, both participating economies of the ABTC, are also seen to have similar arrangements with other APEC members. This seems to indicate that mobility across national borders depends much on social networks, and this is more common in economies where there are ties of nationality and language than where there are no such ties. Australia appears to be an exception in the sense that it only has a visa-free entry arrangement with New Zealand, yet it is a member of the ABTC scheme. This is perhaps an indication of its desire to have greater engagement in Asia and a willingness to allow more migrants into its economy.

Secondly, only four countries — Australia, Canada, Japan and the United States — allow a five-year multiple-entry visa to all or most business travellers. Note that these are advanced nations that presumably are technically capable of handling complex travel procedures. The absence of such capacity and its other associated aspects in the other countries is thus seen as a deterrence to the overall implementation of the ABTC scheme. As already mentioned, this issue is being addressed. However, the severity of the problem can be inferred from Table 1, suggesting that the immediate implementation of the programme may not be forthcoming.

Thirdly, the economies differ substantially in the processing of residency permits. It can be noted that the more advanced economies tend in general to be stricter in accepting longer staying migrants. While these economies tend to be more open to people staying a month, they would impose stricter regulations to more extended residencies. This seems to suggest that these countries may tend to consider in-migrants as possible threats to their economy. At least, in the discussions of the Informal Exports Group on Business Mobility, according to the APEC Secretariat, there are a few overt concerns about the scheme being detrimental to an economy's progress.

As long as this mobility does not cause any negative impact on the economy and is short-term, most of the APEC economies seem to understand the need for technology transfer and the inflow of skills that are otherwise unavailable in an economy. Nonetheless, the momentum for greater business mobility seems to be stalling. Hence, the scope for mobility needs to be expanded and managed well.

Boonprapa, in his response to our questions, suggested downplaying the importance of the ABTC. Instead of viewing this as visa facilitation, the ABTC should be seen merely as an electronic network that will help

TABLE 1 **Business Mobility Regulations and Standards in APEC**

Economies	Short-term Business Visas		Business Residency Service Standards		
	Visa-free	5-yr MEV	Applications: 1 month	Extensions: 1 week	Auto. 3-yr renewal
Australia	1	Yes	No: 6 weeks	No: 4 weeks	1-4 years, not auto.
Brunei	11	No			
Canada	10	Yes	75% within 1 month	No: 4 weeks	3 years, not auto.
Chile	8	No	No: 3 months	No: 3 months	1 year, not auto.
China	2	No	Yes	Yes	1-5 years, not auto.
Hong Kong	15	No	Maybe: 4-6 weeks	No: 2 weeks	2 or 3 years, not auto.
Indonesia	0	No			
Japan	7	Yes	No: 5 weeks	Yes	3 years, not auto.
Korea	15	No	Yes	Yes	3 years, not auto.
Malaysia	14	No			
Mexico	8	No	No: 6 weeks	No: 4-6 weeks	1 year, not auto.
New Zealand	10	No	Maybe: 1-6 weeks	Maybe: 1-6 weeks	3 years, not auto.
Papua New Guinea	0	No			
Philippines	15	Some	No: 2 months	Not needed	Not needed
Singapore	16	No	Yes	No: 2 weeks	1-5 years, not auto.
Chinese Taipei	5	No	Yes		
Thailand	14	No	Yes	No: 1 month	1 year, not auto
United States	5	Yes	Yes	No: 3-4 weeks	1-5 years, not auto.

Notes:
Visa-free: shows the number of other APEC economies to which the economy offers visa-free entry for short-term business travellers.
5-yr MEV: shows whether or not the economy makes available a five-year multiple-entry visa to all or most business travellers, though issuance may not be automatic.
Applications – 1 month: shows whether applications for business residency permits are processed within one month and, if not, how long it takes.
Extensions – 1 week: shows whether extensions of business residency permits are processed within one week and, if not, how long it takes.
Auto. 3 yr. renewal: shows whether three-year renewal of business residency permits is automatically granted and, if not, for how long renewal is granted and whether it is automatic.

SOURCE: Compiled by the APEC Secretariat based on information supplied by member economies. Updated 12 June 1998.

speed up immigration control procedures, mostly for airport checking. However, in his answer to our questions, Ricafort disagreed, noting that the success of some small and medium-scale enterprises hinges on the ability of entrepreneurs to visit and learn from other countries, especially the developed countries. A common acceptance of the ABTC should be pursued, as committed in the IAPs of individual countries. He sees this as a way of "levelling the playing field" or a way of giving every economic sector the opportunity to move across different regions.

Assessment of Strengths and Weaknesses

Unless travel and migration processes are streamlined and standardized across economies, the initiative to enhance business mobility will at best be slow and halting. Fundamentally, labour mobility is the outcome of the market system. The benefits come in the form of greater efficiencies from specialization, from more rapid technology transfer, and more productive allocation of resources, from comparative advantage and from the discipline of competition. Historically, Williamson (1998) has shown that much of the significant factor price convergence in the earlier globalization era was driven by emigration rather than by international trade. Hence, higher business mobility is expected to show up in higher rates of economic growth, causing higher wages and higher returns to capital and leading to higher standards of living, especially for the poorer economies.

However, there is another set of arguments that are political in nature, having to do with political stability and potential for conflict. This argument, which goes beyond the basic premises of the ABTC, is important since economic growth, especially one induced by labour movements, does not necessarily imply stability. While low economic growth and dramatic political movements are linked, economic change and the consequent change in the balance of power among resource owners and in the shifts in state control have often caused clashes in both political and economic policies.

Summers (1999) pointed to an "integration trilemma" which applies very well to the issue of labour mobility. Since every supporter of labour mobility faces the challenge of reconciling general interest with special interest, the challenge lies in achieving the three goals of economic integration or labour mobility: greater resource movement or integration, proper public (macroeconomic) management, and national sovereignty. The problem, however, is that in reconciling any two of these objectives, the rejection of the third is necessary — hence, the "economic integration trilemma". For instance, modern protectionism often resolves this trilemma by emphasizing sovereignty and the need for public management at the expense of greater global integration. Traditional economists, on the other hand, resolve this problem by stressing the benefits of greater integration and national sovereignty, eroding the government's capacity to tax incomes, or to regulate industry. Finally, the "international idealists" would call for emphasizing integration and public policy, with significant impositions on sovereignty.

In an economy that is managed properly to optimize the trade-off between inflation and unemployment, greater labour mobility will not affect the quantity of jobs in the global market — only their sectoral composition. In most economies, adding export jobs and subtracting import jobs raises the average standard of the economies. Yet, enhancing the import sector will also not necessarily be adverse to the economy since it can lead to lower consumer prices, greater competitiveness for producers who use imports, and downward pressure on inflation. Greater business people mobility will not necessarily reduce jobs, whether in export or import industries, if technological improvements and factor specialization are simultaneously enhanced. The key task of APEC in developing labour mobility will then not be focused on reconciling the "integration trilemma", but in addressing the key links between labour mobility, technological innovation, and factor specialization. By improving these links, one can go a long way towards achieving both integration and political sovereignty.

In this case, a more effective and logical way of implementing the objectives of labour mobility is for the programme to develop even further by allowing every citizen of member economies to gain entry to different sectors in the other economies, as trade liberalization, financial integration, and technological transfer are being achieved. Given the important benefits of the joint liberalization of goods and factors of production, and the concomitant exchange of technology, other APEC economies will be strongly encouraged to participate actively in the programme. If this is to be implemented over the long run, then the full fruition of the APEC vision may be realized.

Recommendations

The demand for labour market integration has taken on greater prominence and urgency in recent years in the wake of events in the global financial markets. As the financial crisis lingers, its effects on social sectors have become perceptible, requiring closer attention to cooperation and technical assistance. The challenge for policy-making in the business labour mobility area is to find solutions that can navigate between possibly impractical extremes to build a stronger global labour market.

First, there is a need to increase further the transparency between the domestic and international labour markets, as it is presently implemented. This refers to the establishment of suitable and internationally acceptable travel and migration regulations and processes. Broader support and agreement for codes and standards among the APEC economies should lead to clearer and less fraudulent methods of entry, thereby protecting both the host and sending economies. It is increasingly recognized that the establishment of standardized rules and institutions is a win-win scheme for the global economy and the individual economies. Moreover, less restrictive regulations from the more developed economies are expected to lead to a rapid implementation of this programme. It is generally accepted that the labour markets in more advanced economies have not kept pace with the rapid development of their domestic economy nor with increasing financial liberalization.

Secondly, if short-term migration is generally preferred to long-run residency, then greater emphasis should be placed on the former. This will give each economy the maximum incentive to seek alternatives for an abbreviated, yet more effective, technological transfer than can be realized from longer labour residency, while containing the potential for labour displacement. In the attempt to improve mobility, national sovereignty should also be respected and the creation of support for mobility should not engender a backlash against one's allies. However, these criteria should be balanced against the global need for credible policies that will also generate support for more integration.

Finally, given the already existing well-defined social networks of labour mobility (beyond those created by ABTC), the general direction of the scheme should be the intensification of such networks as more routes for labour movements are developed. In particular, the ASEAN policy of visa-free entries for three weeks for all citizens should be expanded to all APEC economies for consistency. The continued presence of such networks indicates to a large extent their efficiency and their resilience, as well as their ability to integrate varied preferences and institutions into the process. Enhancing these networks — even initially only within some subregions of APEC — will lead to a more stable and viable mobility of labour. Once this is achieved, business can then be tapped to expand these flows to a much larger setting.

References

Okayama, H. "Response to the APEC Business Travel Card Questionnaire of ABAC". Singapore: APEC Secretariat, 2000. Available on the APEC Secretariat Website: <http://www.apecsec.org.sg>

Summers, L. "Distinguished Lecture on Economics in Government: Reflections on Managing Global Integration." *Journal of Economic Perspectives* 13 (1999): 3-8.

Williamson, J. "Globalization, Labor Markets and Policy Backlash in the Past". *Journal of Economic Perspectives* 12 (1998): 51–72.

6

HUMAN RESOURCE DEVELOPMENT IN APEC

JIANREN LU & GLEN TAYLOR

To evaluate the role and distinct contribution of APEC to human resource development (HRD), it is essential to understand the context in which HRD has been institutionalized within the APEC process. From its inception, HRD has been a central APEC focus. In 1993, the Blake Island Leaders' Declaration[1], captured the spirit of this commitment by agreeing:

> … to make an investment in our future generations by establishing an APEC Education Program to develop regional cooperation in higher education, study key regional economic issues, improve worker skills, facilitate cultural and intellectual exchanges, enhance labor mobility and foster understanding of the diversity of our region… to promote cooperation among us in the areas of human resource development and the exchange of management skills and techniques.

To link the broad goals of APEC into coordinated and focused action steps, a method of prioritizing and evaluating initiatives on economic and technical cooperation was defined — it is generally referred to as the "Ecotech framework".[2] The "development of human capital" is one of the six main themes within the Economic and Technical Cooperation

(Ecotech) framework. The goals of economic and technical cooperation as defined in this framework are as follows:

- to attain sustainable growth and equitable development in the Asia-Pacific region;
- to reduce economic disparities among APEC economies;
- to improve the economic and social well-being of the people; and
- to deepen the spirit of community in the Asia-Pacific.

Because its purpose was to develop a coherent process for initiating and managing an increasingly diverse set of actions, the Ecotech framework is intended to establish the means by which economic and technical cooperation can proceed in an effective manner within the APEC process. With that in mind, Ecotech embodies an agreement on the character of APEC economic and technical cooperation initiatives:

- to be goal-oriented with explicit objectives, milestones, and performance criteria;
- to increase the role of the private/business sectors in APEC, not only to participate but also initiate economic and technical cooperation activities in line with APEC goals;
- to combine government actions, private sector projects, and joint public–private activities, with the public sector playing a direct or indirect role in creating and enabling an environment for private sector initiative; and
- to draw on voluntary contributions commensurate with member economies' capabilities and generate direct and broadly shared benefits among APEC member economies to reduce economic disparities in the region.

The Scope of HRD Activities within APEC

Because it cuts across so much of what APEC strives to accomplish through Ecotech, HRD capacity-building is embedded in a wide range of initiatives and projects. To this end, HRD requires a strong emphasis on building networks to share and coordinate efforts where there is an HRD component, as well as to generate effective input from individuals and organizations outside APEC. The same is true for the dissemination of the work products of HRD, which only achieve their full value when they are effectively linked to the efforts of others beyond those directly participating as officials in the APEC process.

The broad intent of HRD within the APEC process is to increase the capacity of member economies to develop the skills of their citizens. HRD capacity-building is intended to enable member economies and their citizens to contribute to economic growth in the APEC region and to share the benefits derived from participation in the development of an open regional economy. The increased importance of knowledge and skills as a driving force in economic development adds additional importance to APEC's HRD capacity-building role.

HRD is a cross-cutting theme in the full spectrum of APEC concerns; all parties and institutions need to co-operate and work together on HRD issues. At present, there are several official channels for economies to work together on HRD issues through the APEC process: APEC HRD Ministerial Meetings, Senior Officials Meetings, HRD Working Group (HRDWG), and APEC fora such as the Ad Hoc Policy Level Group on Small and Medium Enterprises (PLGSME). The HRD Ministerial Meetings held in 1996, 1997 and 1999[3] were responsible for:

- establishing the general principles for HRD policy implementation;
- endorsing the HRD action framework and action plan to promote the growth of HRD in the region;
- defining priority items and programmes; and
- putting HRD-related suggestions forward to the Leaders' Meetings.

Other Ministerial Meetings on Education, Sustainable Development, SME and Science and Technology are involved in many issues and initiatives related to HRD. For example, the Joint Statement from the third meeting of APEC Regional Science and Technology Ministers (1998) emphasized the importance of HRD in the creation of partnerships and networks.

The Human Resource Development Working Group was established in 1990 to cover a broad range of HRD issues, from basic education to industrial training, to leadership and management for small and medium enterprises (SMEs). The HRDWG deals with specific issues and develops specific initiatives concerning HRD directly or indirectly.

Information networks and systems are important to developing human resources. The HRD working group was reorganized in the year 2000 to create more effective and streamlined groupings. The Capacity Building Network (CBN) was created by combining the Network on Human Resource Development in Industrial Technology (HURDIT), and the Business Management Network (BMN). The Education Network (EDNET) was created from the Education Forum (EDFOR). The Labour and Social Protection Network (LSP) derives from the Network on Economic Development Management (NEDM), and the Labour Market Information Group (LMI). The CBN focuses on information on human capacity building, the EDNET focuses on education information, and the LSP focuses on information on labour markets, work-place conditions, and strong social safety nets (see Box 1).

BOX 1

Summary of the Key Initiatives in the HRD Area

HRD has been identified by Leaders as a priority issue for APEC since 1989:

- In the 1991 Seoul Declaration, HRD was identified as an important area for economic and technical cooperation to move towards the goals of sustainable growth and the economic and social well-being of people in the region.
- The 1994 Jakarta Declaration on Framework for HRD set out the objectives, principles, and priorities for HRD in APEC.
- The Action Programme for HRD, as part of the Osaka Action Agenda in November 1995, stated that the goal of HRD is to promote the well-being of all people in the region through economic growth and development. HRD also has an important role to play in liberalizing and facilitating trade and investment.
- The 1996 Declaration on an APEC Framework for Strengthening Economic Cooperation and Development identified HRD as one of the six Leaders' priorities for economic and technical cooperation.
- In the 1998 Kuala Lumpur Declaration, HRD was identified as a key factor towards achieving sustained growth for the 21st century, and Leaders also endorsed the 1998 Kuala Lumpur Action Programme on Skills Development in APEC as a "significant inroad into public-business collaborative partnership in skills development".
- In APEC 2000, HRD is listed as a core element.

HRD Actions Undertaken by Working Groups

HRDWG is responsible for providing suggestions to the HRD Ministerial Meetings, implementing directives from Ministerial Meetings, developing medium-term development strategies and annual work plans, organizing and managing projects and symposiums, and co-ordinating its efforts with other APEC fora and institutions (see Table 1).

At present, the HRDWG has completed and endorsed over one hundred projects at other APEC fora. Some projects have been going on for several years and progress reports have been provided at almost every HRDWG meeting. Such projects include: University Mobility in

Asia and the Pacific (UMAP) by Australia; Japan-APEC Partnership for Education and Training (JAPET) by Japan; APEC Vocational Training Programme and APEC Youth Skill Camp Programme by Korea; Education Hubs by Singapore; and APEC Business Volunteer Programme (APEC BVP) by Thailand.

HRD-related projects undertaken have played the following roles: first, they are helpful in strengthening employment capability, especially among the youth and women, and promoting labour mobility across member economies. Secondly, they are beneficial for member governments to adjust the labour market system and policies, reform the educational system, and improve the work-place through exchange of best practices, and to share experiences and information related to HRD. Thirdly, many projects will contribute to the economic growth of the entire region. New projects undertaken in the past few years are shown in Table 2.

In addition to projects undertaken by the HRDWG, there is often an HRD component in the projects of other working groups. Examples of this are the Fisheries Working Group on-site in-plant training sessions for seafood inspection regimes, and the Industrial Science and Technology (IST) Working Group's Youth Science Festival project. Most of the sectoral working groups also have active human resource activities. The Transportation Working Group has created the steering committee on human resources development while the IST Working Group has identified "improved human resources development" as one of its six key priorities.

Assessment of HRD

The effectiveness of APEC efforts to develop human capital, which has been so important since the inception of the APEC process, is not easy to assess. HRD is not the responsibility of only one working group, and even within the HRD working group, the scope of HRD activities is broad and diverse. What follows is an attempt to identify some of the critical concerns and issues that APEC needs to resolve. For the purpose of this assessment, the issues are divided into two categories: issues that relate to the internal validity of the decision-making process within APEC, and issues that relate to the external relevance of the APEC process.

Concern for the internal validity of the APEC process consumes a great deal of the time and energy for those involved with APEC. A review of APEC reports reinforces this perception. Even serious attempts to critique the effectiveness of HRD using the Ecotech framework proved susceptible to developing a set of recommendations in which all issues are treated as if the solutions reside in fine-tuning internal processes of coordination and communication.[4] While attention was disproportionately directed to improving internal coordination in earlier assessments, there is more concern expressed here for the external relevance of APEC.

TABLE 1 **Types of Co-operative Actions related to HRD**

Types	Contents
Developing projects and annual work-plans	Focusing on labour market policy, the education system and the work-place, etc.
Preparing reports for Ministerial Meetings	Such as HRD and the social effects of the financial crisis
Information construction	Establishing networks including: CBN, EDNET, LSP
Coordinating with other fora and institutions	Providing suggestions to other fora and institutions, avoiding duplication of work, etc.
Strengthening self-management	Moving to an annual meeting, reducing networks from five to three, setting up new criteria for projects, etc.

Weak Internal Coordination of HRD Activities

In terms of individual initiatives, it can be said that HRD activities should include well-designed projects with clear goals, as well as strong support and participation from government, the private sector, and civil society. This is the essence of the Ecotech framework as applied to evaluating and selecting projects. An assessment of individual projects, which is beyond the scope of this review, would no doubt show that many fit this description and contribute to the larger APEC process, and have an impact on market outcomes or policy development. For example, the project on "Innovative Practices in Labour Market Adjustment Policies and Programmes in APEC Member Economies" contributed to the HRD Ministerial Meeting, and the final copy was made available for distribution at the meeting as well as the Leaders' and Ministers' meetings in New Zealand in September 1999. There is also little doubt that the HRDWG is playing a more effective role since making recent adjustments to its internal structure and management process. In order to avoid duplication of work on HRD, the HRDWG is now better able to coordinate its efforts with the other APEC working groups and fora to implement HRD projects.

An assessment of HRD requires more than the consideration of individual projects. It has long been recognized that HRD efforts need some focus to make the best use of resources and to ensure that there is some systematic quality in which the results are more than the sum of their parts. To be effective, HRD initiatives must serve as a catalyst for broader action rather than be the sole solution to all issues of concern in the region.

TABLE 2 **New Network Projects Endorsed by HRDWG from 1998 to 2000**

HRDWG Meeting	APEC Central Funding	Sponsors	TILF Funding	Sponsors	Self-funded	Sponsors
18th	Maintenance of the APEC LMI Database	Australia/ LMI	APEC Experts-Trainers-Executives Workshop on International Quality Assurance Systems	Philippines/ Japan/ BMN	Mutual Recognition of Qualification — Stage III (Engineering) (EDFOR)	Australia
	Integration of Information and Communications Technologies through Teacher Professional Development and Pre-Service Training	Canada/ EDFOR			Best Practices Workshop on School to Work Transition in APEC Member Economies for Youth at Greatest Risk of Unemployment (EDFOR/HURDIT)	Canada
	Trainers Training Programme in Industrial HRD School-Industry Linkages for Industry Workers, Trainers and Supervisors	Philippines/ HURDIT			Alternative Dispute Resolution Executive Education Project (BMN)	Japan
	Application of Total Productive Maintenance (TPM) in Small and Medium Industry	Thailand/ HURDIT			APEC White Collar Training Programme on Production and Material Handling Management under the Total Management System (BMN/HURDIT)	Japan

TABLE 2 (*Cont'd*)

HRDWG Meeting	APEC Central Funding	Sponsors	TILF Funding	Sponsors	Self-funded	Sponsors
	Successful Practices in Human Resources Development in the Workplace: Contributions from Labour, Management, and Government	Canada/ NEDM			Cross-Member Seminar on Social Development and Human Resources Development in the APEC Member Economies (NEDM)	Japan
	Chief Human Resources Officer (CHRO) Network Project Phase II	Thailand/ BMN			APEC Youth Skill Camp Programme (HURDIT)	Korea
					Cross-Cultural Comparison on Open-Learning System in APEC member economies (EDFOR)	Korea
					Exchange of Education Professional among APEC Member Economies (EDFOR)	Korea
					Workshop on Work-based Education and Training: Reconsidering the Role of Government (NEDM)	New Zealand

TABLE 2 (*Cont'd*)

HRDWG Meeting	APEC Central Funding	Sponsors	TILF Funding	Sponsors	Self-funded Economic Restructuring	Sponsors Chinese
					and Labour Market Dynamics (NEDM)	Taipei
					Achieving High Performing Schools (EDFOR)	USA/ China
19th					APEC Forum on Human Resource Development (HURDIT)	Japan
20th	Seminar on Capacity-Building of APEC Entrepreneurs on International Business Management	China/ BMN	Alternative Dispute — Executive Education Project	Japan/ BMN	Social Safety Net Programmes in Selected APEC Economies 1997-2000	Canada/ NEDM
	IT Enablement for Trainers in the New Millennium (Brunei Darussalam)	HURDIT			HRD for Venture Business in APEC	Japan/ BMN
	Skill Shortage Training Needs and HRD Strategies of Multinational Enterprises	HURDIT			Workshop on International Migration and Human Resource Development in the APEC Member Economies	Japan/ NEDM

TABLE 2 (*Cont'd*)

HRDWG Meeting	APEC Central Funding	Sponsors	TILF Funding	Sponsors	Self-funded	Sponsors
	Achieving High Performing Schools: Using Measurement to Manage Improvement	China / EDFOR			APEC Forum on Human Resources Development — Vocational Training Policies Toward 21st Century	Japan/ HURDIT
	KDI School as an Education Hub	Korea/ EDFOR				
	Global Advantage through People: Human Resources Management Policies and Practice in 11 APEC Economies	Brunei/ HURDIT				
	APEC Youth Networking: Youth Preparation	Thailand/ EDFOR				
	Corporate & Non-profit Governance and Restoration of Prosperity of APEC Economies	U.S.A/ BMN				

TABLE 2 (*Cont'd*)

HRDWG Meeting	APEC Central Funding	Sponsors	TILF Funding	Sponsors	Self-funded	Sponsors
21th					Innovation and Best Practices in Building Educational and Labour Market Capability for Indigenous Peoples	NEDM
					Best Practices for Eliminating the Worst Forms of Child Labour and Providing Educational Opportunities	NEDM
					Workshop on International Migration and Human Resource Development in the APEC Member Economies — Phase II: Symposium on International Migration and Structural Change in APEC Member Economies	NEDM

TABLE 2 (*Cont'd*)

HRDWG Meeting	APEC Central Funding	Sponsors	TILF Funding	Sponsors	Self-funded	Sponsors
	Management Consultancy for Small to Medium-Sized Enterprises	PFP				
	International Business Financing	PFPs				
	APEC Speakers Bureau on Standards-Based Management	BMN/ CTI				
22nd	The Seminar on the Best Practices for Professional Development of Vocational Teachers Among APEC Economies	Thailand/ EDNET	Capacity Building Programme for Trade and Investment Insurance Practitioners (CBP TIIP)	Philippines/ CB	Management Consultancy for Small and Medium-Sized Enterprises	Japan/ CBN
	The Use of Information Technology in a Learning Society	Singapore/ EDNET			International Trade Financing	Japan/ CBN
	APEC Cyber Education Cooperation Project	Korea/ EDNET			New Directions in Student Assessment in APEC Economies	USA/ China/ EDNET

TABLE 2 (*Cont'd*)

HRDWG Meeting	APEC Central Funding	Sponsors	TILF Funding	Sponsors	Self-funded	Sponsors
Australia/	Innovation and Best Practice in Building Educational and Labour Market Capability for Indigenous Peoples	New Zealand/ Canada/ LSP			The APEC Architect Project	EDNET
	Helping Business Respond to Change: Innovations in Labour-Management-Government Cooperation	USA/ LSP			Workshop on International Migration and HRD, Phase II	Japan/ Chinese Taipei/ LSP
	APEC Forum on Cross-Cultural Understanding of the Implementation of Standards and Accreditation in Supply-Chain Management	Philippines/ USA/ CBN			APEC Forum on HRD: HRD in Manufacturing Industry	Japan/ LSP
					Best Practices for Eliminating the Worst Forms of Child Labour and Providing Educational Opportunities	USA/ LSP

SOURCE: Summary Conclusions from the 17th to the 22nd HRDWG Meetings, 1998–2000.

Inadequate initiation of APEC projects among developing member economies also warrants careful consideration. As shown in Table 2, most projects are directed or participated by APEC developed member economies. However, to some degree, APEC developing member economies need to strengthen human resources and increase their productivity more than the developed economies, especially to meet challenges from the financial crisis and the growing importance of the knowledge-based economy. It is vitally important to increase their participation in HRD projects.

Weak External Support for APEC

Developing human resources is a common challenge throughout the entire Asia-Pacific region. It is a challenge of such immense proportions that it is difficult at times to discern where the specific value-added of APEC can best be focused. HRD is like a public good in which the costs and benefits may result in under-investment by the private sector. Unless there is an increase in the funding for HRD and an improved ability to focus resources for maximum impact on economic development, the impact of the resources that APEC directs to HRD will remain superficial. This also highlights why APEC needs to engage the private sector more fully. If the economies are not willing to commit the resources to address HRD issues, it is hard to understand why the private sector will want to be involved.

APEC activities lack relevance or are poorly linked to outside interests. A relatively small group of APEC insiders takes the time to concern themselves with APEC, and when issues do arise, it is not surprising that the ones most energetically pursued reflect the interests of the people in the APEC process. Despite the use of the Ecotech framework, it appears that the goal of increased private sector participation and initiation of activities is not being met. Nor is there much evidence of successful efforts to combine government actions, private sector projects and joint public–private activities with the public sector playing a direct or indirect role in creating and enabling an environment for private sector initiative. Participation in the APEC process needs to be more attractive to the private sector. The time-consuming nature of APEC procedures, including the onerous guidelines for projects, the impenetrable maze of acronyms, and APEC's organizational structure as well as the high cost of managing APEC projects, all combine to actively discourage private sector participation.

Failure to intently pursue external relevance weakens other aspects of APEC's effectiveness. Governments are sensitive to their constituencies, and it is far from clear how much public awareness and support there is for APEC. If APEC is seen as a place where meetings are long on form and short on substance — in other words, all talk and no action — it is likely that external support will remain weak. If action is intended to take the form of new policy initiatives by governments, and if no new initiatives are forthcoming, even those who are close to the APEC process cannot help but view it with some scepticism. If the goal is to generate contributions commensurate with member economies' capabilities for the shared benefit of APEC members, the ability to generate a strong external constituency by the more wealthy economies is a fundamental first step. This is where the resources must come from. If APEC lacks public credibility it will also suffer from a lack of political will and financial support.

Limitations of this Assessment

The assessment presented here is based on a very limited response to an APIAN survey. The lack of response to the survey may itself be an indication of an unwillingness to express an opinion, or simple disinterest. The conclusions are based on a review of the Leaders' and Ministerial Declarations as well as of existing projects and personal experience as a project participant, organizer, and overseer. Informal discussions were held with several representatives from APEC economies and additional input was obtained from the APIAN workshop in Singapore. A prior assessment of HRD presented to the APEC Ministerial Meeting in 1999[5] was also reviewed.

Conclusion

The scope of HRD activities has expanded substantially since the founding of APEC in 1989. The internal effectiveness of HRD depends heavily on the use of coordination mechanisms within the APEC process. By implementing the Ecotech framework and by restructuring the HRD working group, progress has been made in this area. However, the external effectiveness of HRD depends heavily on the engagement of the private sector and partnerships between the public and private sectors. The lack of progress in this area may be due to inadequate effort from member economies to stimulate and promote external initiatives and participation. The relevance of APEC suffers from a lack of this engagement.

For HRD to achieve its potential as a catalyst within the APEC process, external effectiveness must be given top priority, specifically:

1. promote private sector engagement in the APEC process;
2. simplify the APEC process and project management structure to make participation more transparent, easier to comprehend, and less time-consuming to engage in;
3. build external constituencies around relevant and critical issues;
4. develop policies and encourage member economies to implement them to demonstrate that APEC is not "all talk, no action"; and
5. commit resources to form public-private partnerships.

The lack of an APEC strategy or even a coherent pattern in the many HRD activities is a recurring theme. Merely supporting projects that reflect the current interests of active members may generate innovative approaches to HRD issues, but it remains unclear how effective APEC HRD efforts can be so long as external support remains weak. External relevance is the key challenge facing HRD in the APEC process.

Notes

1. Asia-Pacific Economic Cooperation, "Blake Island Economic Leaders Declaration" (Singapore: APEC Secretariat, 1993).
2. Asia-Pacific Economic Cooperation, "Declaration on an Asia-Pacific Economic Cooperation Framework for Strengthening Economic Cooperation and Development, Manila, Philippines, 1996" (Singapore: APEC Secretariat, 1996).
3. Asia-Pacific Economic Cooperation, HRD Ministerial Statements: Manila,1996; Seoul, 1997; Washington, 1999 (Singapore: APEC Secretariat).
4. Asia-Pacific Economic Cooperation, "Developing Human Capital — Sub-Committee on Ecotech Coordination Paper". Annex 6 of the ESC Report to the APEC Ministerial Meeting, Auckland, 1999 (Singapore: APEC Secretariat, 1999).
5. Ibid.

References

Asia-Pacific Economic Cooperation. APEC Joint Ministerial Statements from 1989–1999. Available at <http://www.apecsec.org.sg>.

———. APEC Leaders' Declarations 1993–1999. Available at <http://www.apecsec.org.sg>.

———. "Declaration: A Human Resources Development Framework for the Asia-Pacific Economic Cooperation". Jakarta, 1994

———. "Action Programme for Human Resources Development". Osaka, 1995.

———. "Declaration on an Asia-Pacific Economic Cooperation Framework for Strengthening Economic Cooperation and Development". Manila, 1996. Available at <http://www.apecsec.org.sg>.

———. Joint Ministerial Statements from APEC Education Ministerial (1992 and 2000) and HRD Ministerial Meetings (1996, 1997 and 1999)

———. "HRD WG Statement of Medium Term Strategic Priorities". Available at <http://www.apecsec.org.sg>.

———. "Summary Conclusions from the 17th to the 22nd HRDWG Meetings, 1998–2000".

———. "Developing Human Capital - Sub-Committee on ECOTECH Coordination Paper". Annex 6 of the ESC Report to the APEC Ministerial Meeting, Auckland, 1999.

7

THE APEC FOOD SYSTEM IN 2000
A Case Study

ROBERT SCOLLAY

Introduction

The insertion of "comprehensiveness" as one of the nine principles of APEC liberalization set out in the Osaka Action Agenda was designed to make clear that the trade liberalization envisaged in APEC's Bogor Declaration is to cover all sectors, including agriculture. Computable general equilibrium (CGE) analyses of APEC liberalization typically show that liberalization of agricultural trade accounts for 50–70 per cent of the economic welfare gains potentially available from the achievement of APEC's Bogor liberalization objective (Scollay and Gilbert 2000). Agriculture has also received attention in APEC's Economic and Technical Cooperation (Ecotech) programme, through the work of the Agricultural Technical Cooperation Experts' Group (ATC EG). Agriculture was also an important focus of APEC's FEEEP (food, energy, environment, economic growth and population) initiative.

It has become clear that the existence of large potential welfare gains from agricultural trade liberalization is not sufficient to motivate APEC-wide liberalization in this sector. Substantial political economy obstacles in a number of APEC member economies will have to be overcome before successful liberalization can realistically be expected. Perhaps the most effective way to overcome these obstacles is through measures designed to improve productivity in the agricultural sector, thereby offsetting the negative impact on agricultural incomes that might otherwise be one of the consequences of agricultural trade liberalization (Gilbert, Scollay and Wahl 2000). This suggests the need for an integrated approach to the agricultural sector within APEC, involving elements of both APEC's TILF (Trade and Investment Liberalization and Facilitation) and Ecotech programmes.

The APEC Food System (AFS) proposal put forward by the APEC Business Advisory Council (ABAC) was designed to offer such an integrated approach. The AFS proposal envisages a robust regional food system to

- efficiently link together food producers, processors and consumers;
- harness the resources of the region to more securely meet consumers' food needs; and
- maximize the contribution of the food sector to the wealth and prosperity of all economies.

In September 1999, APEC Ministers adopted a report on the APEC Food System. A few days later, APEC Economic Leaders endorsed the recommendations of that report on the development of rural infrastructure, dissemination of technological advances and food production and processing, and promotion of trade in food products. The Leaders instructed Ministers to implement the recommendations, noting that "a robust regional food system .... is a vital contribution to meeting the goals of APEC".

The purpose of this chapter is to review APEC's performance in implementing the Leaders' instruction during the year 2000.

The AFS Recommendations

A unique feature of the APEC Food System is the emphasis on the need for an integrated approach incorporating each of the elements of development of rural infrastructure, dissemination of technological advances and food production and processing, and promotion of trade in food products. Reflecting this, the recommendations endorsed by the Leaders call for progress to be made across a broad spectrum of activities. They include recommendations that

- the Human Resources Development Working Group should place high priority on addressing the issue of rural education, and member economies undertake cooperative measures with non-government, non-profit organizations to improve the availability of rural education;

- the Infrastructure Workshop's joint initiatives in infrastructure development be actively encouraged by, and the benefits of these initiatives communicated to, member economies;
- the APEC Investment Experts' Group, in conjunction with the World Bank, Inter-American Development Bank, Asian Development Bank (ADB), and Food and Agriculture Organization (FAO) of the United Nations, and other bodies as appropriate, investigate new and innovative ways to attract the investment necessary to build facilities and rehabilitate existing rural infrastructure;
- the Small and Medium Enterprises Policy Level Group could undertake and intensify work on the three areas of cooperation identified by ABAC's APEC Food System proposal;
- relevant APEC fora, including the Committee on Trade and Investment, Economic and Technical Sub-Committee, and the ATC EG should continue to undertake and intensify their work on trade facilitation, economic and technical cooperation, and capacity building on food-related issues, including the following:
  - — providing clear, predictable and easily understood food regulatory frameworks and standards;
  - — according priority to those projects that facilitate the growth of regional trade in food products and improve the technical infrastructure of developing economies;
  - — providing progress reports to the Senior Officials Meeting (SOM) on the endorsement of existing initiatives, such as the Food Mutual Recognition Arrangement;
  - — furthering cooperation in research and development, and dissemination of food-related technology;
  - — building partnerships between the public and business/private sectors in technical cooperation to further food technology transfer, and improving training facilities, and training programmes;
  - — fostering environmentally sound agricultural practices; and
  - — maintaining an awareness of and contributing to international developments in research and policies related to genetically modified foods, and intensifying science-based approaches to the introduction and use of biotechnology products.
- APEC member economies should continue to ensure full and faithful implementation of the commitments on food arising from the Uruguay Round of multilateral trade negotiations;
- APEC member economies, in line with the Osaka Action Agenda and noting ABAC's call for the elimination of unnecessary impediments to trade in food products ahead of the Bogor goals, should:
  - — provide greater specificity in their Individual Action Plans on

how they are going to meet the long-term Bogor goals in the food sector;
- — actively and constructively participate in the forthcoming World Trade Organization (WTO) negotiations on agriculture to consider tariffs and non-tariff measures further in the context of Article 20 of the WTO's Agreement on Agriculture; and
- — in the forthcoming negotiations on agriculture, convey to the WTO membership APEC's support for the abolition of agricultural export subsidies and unjustifiable export prohibitions and restrictions.

- SOM, through relevant fora, should provide annual reports to Ministers on the progress made by APEC member economies in building a robust APEC Food System.

The APEC Food System as endorsed by the APEC Leaders thus comprises an ambitious and wide-ranging programme of activities. Fulfilment of the Leaders' instructions requires both the development of existing activities already being pursued by APEC in its TILF and Ecotech programmes, and the extension of APEC activities into new areas.

Scope of the Review

Given the far-reaching and comprehensive nature of the AFS recommendations, it is to be expected that implementation would take time to gather momentum. Nevertheless, it is possible to identify areas where substantive progress has already been made in the first year of implementation, and other areas where implementation has lagged behind.

Where possible, comments are also made on the effectiveness of implementation in specific areas. Questionnaires were circulated in mid-2000 to selected experts in the APEC economies seeking assessments of effectiveness. However, very few completed questionnaires were returned. In part, this may reflect the fact that implementation of the APEC Food System was then in its very early stages. Work programmes in some areas had yet to get under way, and it may also have been premature to assess effectiveness in some areas where initial progress had been made. Less encouragingly, the lack of response may also indicate that awareness of the APEC Food System and its requirements and implications remained somewhat limited among many APEC member economies.

International Actions

APEC Infrastructure Workshop: The RISE Project

The APEC Infrastructure Workshop has collaborated with the PECC Food and Agriculture forum in a project entitled "Regional Integration for Sustainable Economies" (RISE). This project seeks to play a catalytic role in the development of non-metropolitan regions by encouraging and facilitating the formulation of integrated packages of sound, well-balanced economic and infrastructure development programmes, with each element of the package financed as appropriate by private investment or public funding.

As originally conceived, the programme contained a strong element of exploratory study and information-sharing. The emphasis quickly shifted, however, to the implementation of pilot programmes to provide practical demonstrations of the feasibility and value of the RISE concept of an integrated approach to development.

The RISE approach is based on identification and support for regional growth centres (RGCs). RGCs are expected to have already formulated initial proposals which demonstrate, first, full commitment to providing a conducive framework for infrastructure support to rural/regional development, agricultural production, and rural income generation, and secondly, the existence of a set of productive sector and infrastructure support investment projects which provide a basis for rapid engagement and assistance. RISE missions, comprising representatives from both the private sector and multilateral agencies such as the World Bank and the Asian Development Bank (ADB), work with the RGCs to expand, refine, and develop the proposals, through a series of steps, including consultation and pre-commercial review, until ultimately the proposals, and arrangements for their financing, are in the form of a balanced development plan suitable for implementation. The expectation is that the proposals would include assistance and facilitation measures for specific infrastructure, capacity building, and productive sector investments and for specific trade initiatives, as well as provisions for cooperation and assistance where necessary in managing the ongoing implementation of the development plan.

Jiangmen City (Quangdong Province) in the Pearl River delta of China, and Manado-Bitung on the island of Sulawesi in Indonesia were chosen as the RGCs for the pilot programmes. This allowed the RISE concept to be tested in two settings which differed markedly from each other in terms of the stability or otherwise of the political environment, and of the nature and extent of the logistical difficulties that needed to be overcome.

The collaboration between Jiangmen City and RISE experts has made substantial headway. Nearly twenty projects have been identified, including both commercial projects and infrastructure support projects. Considerable progress has been made in refining the projects. A number of international corporations are engaged in the initiative, and some initial investment commitments have been made. World Bank and ADB experts have been involved at several points in the planning process. Work has continued on planning for the ongoing implementation of the project, and guidance has been sought on procedural and technical aspects of applying for ADB support.

Progress has been less rapid in the case of the Manado-Bitung project because of a combination of factors, including resource constraints faced by the local partners, uncertainties generated by the changing political environment, and the need to overcome logistic and communication problems of a much more serious nature than those which existed in Jiangmen City. Despite these difficulties, RISE coordinators report that commitment to the RISE initiative remains firm among the local partners in Manado-Bitung, and that the elements are in place to bring this pilot project to a successful conclusion. Thus, the Manado-Bitung project demonstrates the potential for the RISE approach to succeed even in relatively difficult local conditions.

The two RISE pilot projects have demonstrated the potential contribution of RISE to the development of non-metropolitan areas in developing APEC economies. The question that must be faced now is whether to move beyond the pilot stage and install RISE as a leading agent of rural development in the region. In making this decision APEC will need to assess not only the outcome of the two pilot projects, but also the likely demand in the region for RISE-type initiatives and the level of commitment of resources that will be needed to expand RISE to meet that demand. The two pilot projects will need to be multiplied many times over if RISE is to make a substantial difference to the outlook for rural development on a region-wide basis.

Earlier indications of interest in the establishment of RGCs were received from a number of APEC economies, including the Philippines, Vietnam, Malaysia, Mexico, and Papua New Guinea. This provides some basis for confidence that a substantial demand for RISE-type initiatives may develop once the results of the two pilot projects have been more widely communicated.

Expanding RISE will be a major challenge for APEC. While reports from the pilot projects have indicated the potential of RISE, they have also suggested that RISE will not be sustainable in the longer term unless some significant problems can be overcome. One issue is the level of commitment by APEC economies. Although resources allocated to the RISE pilot projects were relatively large by APEC standards, they were barely sufficient for the purpose and then only because of the substantial amount of *pro bono* work undertaken by some RISE experts. Participation in the pilot projects by APEC economies was poor: only four APEC economies (and one non-APEC economy) had representative participation in the Jiangmen City project, and only one in Manado-Bitung. It is true that it was always envisaged that the major part of the resources needed to implement RISE-based development would come from the private sector and the multilateral financial institutions, but resources from the latter have proved much more difficult to mobilize than had been expected, and serious difficulties have arisen in meeting eligibility criteria. Because of the integrated nature of RISE developments, a failure to secure funding from the ADB or World Bank for essential infrastructure development may in turn have an inhibiting effect on private sector investment.

If RISE is to become a major instrument of the APEC Food System, it is likely that APEC will need to play a catalytic role for some considerable time to come, until eventually RISE may hopefully become self-sustaining. At this stage, however, the commitment of APEC resources to RISE does not extend beyond the two pilot projects. It is difficult to see how the momentum of RISE can be sustained unless APEC economies, both individually and collectively, are prepared to commit substantial additional resources to the initiative for a further period.

Agricultural Technical Cooperation Experts' Group (ATCEG)

The 2000 work programme of the ATCEG responded to the APEC Food System recommendations in a number of areas, particularly agricultural financing, technology transfer, and biotechnology. Earlier ATCEG work in other areas — for example, the 1999 workshop on sustainable agriculture and environmental issues — may also have the potential to be developed further in response to the AFS recommendations.

Agricultural Financing

In September 2000, the ATCEG ran a training course on agricultural finance. The objective of the course was to contribute to the promotion of farmer-owned cooperative farm credit systems and to assist the agricultural finance institutes in undertaking major reforms. The objective was to be achieved principally by familiarizing participants with Japanese agricultural policy and the Japanese approach to agricultural finance.

Representatives of ten APEC economies, including Japan itself, participated in the training course.

In relation to agricultural finance, the approach of the ATCEG complements that of the RISE project. Communicating the experience of developed APEC economies such as Japan in this area is useful for other APEC economies. At the same time, the RISE project seeks to respond to agricultural sector financing needs identified on the basis of practical experience in the field in developing APEC economies. It may be useful to explore the merits of establishing a linkage between the two programmes in order to make it easier for APEC member economies to draw on the full range of experience available in this area.

Technology Transfer

The first APEC workshop on Agriculture Technology Transfer and Training (ATTT) was convened in Jakarta, Indonesia, in January 2000. The objectives of the workshop were to develop better understanding of the current state of ATTT, to draw lessons for the prioritization of ATTT activities, and to formulate a joint research and training programme. The workshop was attended by representatives of thirteen APEC economies and by the FAO. The workshop provided an opportunity for the exchange of information among the participating economies, and also drew up an action plan for future implementation.

The action plan emphasized information exchange and networking, implementation of specific technology transfer initiatives and training programmes, and the development of joint research programmes. Another workshop was to be held in early 2001. Included in the proposed follow-up activities is the establishment of an APEC Agriculture Technology Training Clearing House and an APEC website on ATTT.

The first ATTT workshop demonstrated much enthusiasm among the participants, as indicated by the variety of interesting and potentially useful proposals put forward. The challenge for the future will be to channel this initial momentum into the development of a coherent and effective programme.

Biotechnology

The directive from the Leaders to implement the recommendations of the APEC Food System, together with a specific directive from the Ministers on the issue of biotechnology, gave additional impetus to the existing work programme of the ATCEG in this area. The fourth biotechnology workshop was held in Vancouver, Canada, in October 2000, and there are tentative plans to hold more workshops in 2001 and 2002.

Included in the objectives of the biotechnology programme are to enhance information exchange in the area of biotechnology research and technological transfer, to build greater understanding of bio-safety issues, to provide a link between commercial development and public perceptions, and to intensify the adoption of science-based approaches to the introduction and use of biotechnology. For 2000 and in the medium term, the main emphasis of the ATCEG in this area has been on technical cooperation and capacity-building, focusing especially on the development of transparent and science-based national approaches for risk assessment and risk management, and on encouraging effective communications approaches, thereby enhancing public awareness and understanding of biotechnology.

At the request of the Ministers, the ATCEG also prepared during 2000 a report on APEC activities in the area of biotechnology. In addition to outlining the history of APEC's endeavours to come to grips with biotechnology issues, the report also provides recommendations which reflect the future intentions of the ATCEG in this area. These recommendations were endorsed by the Ministers, as well as the Senior Officials Meeting. The report also gave detailed information on activities related to agriculture and food biotechnology in other international fora. The ATCEG appears well-placed to complement other international efforts in this area, and to provide "added value" in the APEC context.

Standards and Conformance Subcommittee

The Standards and Conformance Subcommittee (SCSC) of the APEC Committee on Trade and Investment (CTI) has developed a mutual recognition agreement (MRA) for food products (the APEC Food MRA) and an Arrangement on the Exchange of Information on Food Recalls. As at January 2000, seven APEC member economies had notified their intention to participate in the APEC Food MRA and two economies had notified their intention to participate in the Arrangement on Food Recalls. Three participating economies are required before the latter arrangement can enter into force. The SCSC 2000 work programme included the provision to encourage more member economy participation in both arrangements.

The APEC Food MRA is a voluntary mechanism designed to facilitate trade by minimizing food inspection controls at the point of entry into importing economies on the basis of assurances provided through pre-export conformity assessment using officially recognized inspection and certification systems, and by establishing a mechanism for resolving issues which may disrupt trade. The APEC Food MRA comprises, first, an umbrella arrangement which contains the general provisions applicable to all products and sectors intended to be covered by the

APEC Food MRA, and secondly, sectoral arrangements, which are the implementing elements pertaining to specific foods or food product sectors. The umbrella arrangement does not require participating member economies to enter into sectoral arrangements; however, it encourages participants to enter into a process of confidence-building and closer cooperation which may lead to their eventual participation in specific sectoral arrangements. The APEC Food MRA is thus a flexible, enabling, non-coercive arrangement which allows members to proceed with implementation at their own pace. Its practical implementation, however, depends on the adoption of sectoral arrangements by individual member economies.

The SCSC 2000 work programme also included the implementation of the 2000 TILF Sustainable Development on Research on Food Labelling Laws, Regulations and Standards in APEC member economies. The SCSC also indicated its intention to participate in the CTI Ad Hoc Task Force on Trade Facilitation.

Other Activities

Work by the Marine Resources Conservation Working Group (MRC WG) on the "Management of Red Tide and Harmful Algal Blooms in the APEC Region" provides a basis for helping each APEC economy to develop a scientific and regulatory infrastructure for dealing with this issue. In 2000, the MRC WG launched a three-year project on "Development and Validation of Analytical Methods, Standards and Reference Materials for Seafood Product Safety and Certification", beginning in May 2000. This project will assist member economies to establish science-based sanitary/phytosanitary standards on seafood products.

No information was obtained on the APEC Food System-related initiatives launched by the Human Resources Development Working Group, the Investment Experts Group, or the Small and Medium Enterprises Policy Level Group.

APEC member economies participated in the discussions on agriculture at the abortive WTO Ministerial meeting in Seattle in December 1999. During these discussions, however, APEC was unable to act cohesively as a group in support of the positions implied by the APEC Food System recommendations. Nevertheless, by calling for the elimination of subsidies on agricultural exports, APEC added its voice to the growing number of countries and country groups which have adopted this position, thereby adding to the increasing international pressure for a definitive resolution of the export subsidies issue.

Individual Actions

Collective actions are often indispensable to the achievement of given APEC objectives, particularly in the Ecotech area, and in all cases can play a vital preparatory and supportive role. However, there are also many cases in which the achievement of APEC objectives depends ultimately on individual actions by APEC member economies. In the case of the APEC Food System recommendations, actions are particularly needed to give effect to the recommendations relating to the promotion of trade in food products.

The 2000 Individual Action Plans were the first to be tabled since APEC Leaders mandated the implementation of Ministers' recommendations for the APEC Food System. They, thus, provide an important test of the extent to which individual member economies are responding to those recommendations.

It is perhaps not encouraging that only nine of the twenty-one APEC members apparently responded to a request by the SOM's Chair for information on the steps they are taking or plan to take to implement the APEC Food System.

Conclusions and Recommendations

The APEC Food System proposal holds out a vision of an integrated and comprehensive approach by APEC economies to policies relating to the food and agriculture sectors.

So far, however, activity by the APEC economies in this area has more of the appearance of a scattered set of uncoordinated actions. Very few collective actions appear to have been undertaken as a direct response to the Leaders' mandate to implement the Ministers' APEC Food System recommendations. More often, the actions identified in the report involve the continuation or, in some cases, further development of existing programmes. In a few cases, new initiatives have emerged from an APEC forum such as the ACTEG, or by committed groups of experts, such as those associated with the RISE project. Generally, however, APEC appears to be finding it difficult to respond to the APEC Food System recommendations, in cases where they do not have a clear relation to existing programmes.

The RISE project is one initiative designed to generate new developments of a tangible nature. The APEC Food MRA and the Arrangement on Food Recalls constitute implementable international agreements. However, the most common activities identified in this report consist of workshops, seminars, and other forms of information exchange.

The pooling of knowledge through information exchange is a valuable activity. The APEC Food System proposal, however, aspires to achieve tangible results. To do this, a combination of results-oriented collective actions and individual actions is indispensable.

It does not, of course, follow that APEC should assume sole responsibility for the implementation of the AFS recommendations. This is not feasible, given the level of resources currently available to APEC, nor is it probably desirable. Nevertheless, for the AFS proposal to retain credibility, there must exist at least an outline plan indicating the full range of specific developments which are expected to follow from the implementation of the AFS, and also where the responsibility lies for the implementation of each development, detailing the contributions which various APEC fora are expected to make to the process, and the ways in which APEC actions will be coordinated with the actions of other agencies to ensure that the full potential of the AFS proposal is realized. Among other things, this would provide the individual APEC fora with a clearer understanding of how their work is expected to contribute to the overall implementation of the AFS.

A greater emphasis on planning the implementation of the AFS will also provide scope for more careful analysis of the specific needs of APEC members, and for the design of programmes to meet those needs in the most effective way possible.

It is imperative to take a longer term perspective. For example, the RISE project appeared at the end of the 2000 work programme to be at risk because the APEC-funded component of the project, which involved a commitment for one year only, had been concluded, and no provision appeared to have been made or responsibility allocated for the ongoing development of the project. Some individual APEC fora now have programmes which extend over considerably longer periods. For the effective implementation of the AFS, it is necessary that a longer-term planning horizon be adopted for the System itself.

The adoption of an overall planning approach and a longer term perspective will assist in the identification of gaps, which are not being covered by the existing programmes of national or multilateral agencies, and which APEC itself does not currently have the resources to fill. In such cases, members will have to face the question of whether the most effective approach will be to expand the activities of the existing agencies or to provide additional resources to APEC so that appropriate APEC fora can fill the gaps identified.

To realize the concept of an integrated, comprehensive policy approach, it is essential that the APEC economies complement collective actions with individual actions which demonstrate a credible level of commitment to the trade element of the AFS proposal.

Individual actions may consist of unilateral measures undertaken by individual APEC economies, implementation of commitments arising out of WTO negotiations, or fresh commitments to implement APEC voluntary arrangements, such as the APEC Food MRA. A review of the state of play in each of these areas of individual action is likely to be a useful exercise. The review will, of course, show that WTO negotiations on agriculture are making little progress. Thus, the impetus for agricultural liberalization, which had earlier been anticipated from the WTO process, appears unlikely to materialize in the short term. This places added importance on unilateral actions by individual APEC members and on the implementation of commitments to APEC voluntary arrangements. The level of commitment by the APEC economies to sectoral implementation of the APEC Food MRA can be critically examined as part of an overall review of the level of commitment to the trade element of the AFS, demonstrated by the latest Individual Action Plans.

Any shortcomings in the level of commitment to the AFS identified in an analysis of individual actions can be addressed through the established APEC procedures for reviewing Individual Action Plans, designed to generate "peer pressure" for improved performance.

References

Scollay, R. and J. Gilbert. "Measuring the Gains from APEC Trade Liberalization: An Overview of CGE Assessments". *World Economy* 23, no. 2 (2000): 175–97.

Gilbert, J., R. Scollay, and T. Wahl. "The APEC Food System: Implications for Agricultural and Rural Development Policy". *Developing Economies* 38, no. 3 (September 2000): 308–29.

8

APEC'S GOALS IN INDUSTRIAL SCIENCE AND TECHNOLOGY

NEANTRO SAAVEDRA-RIVANO

Summary of Key Initiatives

The main statement of APEC initiatives and goals regarding industrial science and technology is the APEC Agenda for Science and Technology Industry Co-operation into the 21st Century, approved by the Leaders' Meeting in Kuala Lumpur (1998). The Agenda gives further precision to the Mexico Declaration that was announced in Mexico City (October 1998) by the Ministers of APEC economies responsible for science and technology (SAT).

It presents a vision of

> a dynamic and prosperous Asia-Pacific region built on the development and application of industrial science and technology which supports economic growth and improves quality of life, while safeguarding the environment and the natural resources necessary for economic sustainability. The successful development, application and commercialization of industrial science and technology will depend upon the ability of APEC economies to create a strong open innovation system and to work co-operatively to catalyze the development of strong sustainable regional S&T networks and partnership.

This vision is to be promoted through five mechanisms:

1. Improved availability and access to information;
2. Improved human resource development;
3. Improved business climate;
4. Enhanced policy dialogue and review; and
5. Facilitation of networks and partnerships.

A Brief Methodological Note

This report will assess the actions taken at the international and member economy levels. A questionnaire was prepared and sent to experts on industrial science and technology in a number of APEC economies ("issue experts"). Five replies to this questionnaire were received — from Australia, Korea, Singapore, and Thailand, in addition to a reply from the APEC Secretariat. The assessment was then elaborated on, taking as primary inputs the replies to the questionnaire as well as information available from the APEC Secretariat. Due consideration was given to the twelve technology areas singled out for collaborative and joint research activities by the APEC Agenda for Science and Technology Industry Co-operation into the 21st Century. These are listed below:

- Biotechnology
- Environmental and Cleaner Production Technologies
- Communication
- Information Technologies/Electronics
- Advanced Materials
- Mechatronics
- Transportation
- Resource Management Technology
- Energy
- Sustainable Agriculture
- Emergency Preparedness and Climate Prediction
- Exploitation of Natural Resources

Actions Taken at the International Level

The Industrial Science and Technology Working Group (ISTWG) is the operational forum of APEC dealing with this sector, and as such it is responsible for developing activities that substantiate the vision spelled out in the APEC Agenda for Science and Technology Industry Cooperation. The Senior Officials Meeting (SOM) Sub-Committee on Economic and Technical Cooperation, which in turn reports to the Ministerial Meetings, supervises its work. Perhaps the most useful action taken by the ISTWG has been the creation of the APEC Science and

Technology Web (AST Web) that provides tools for the flow of information about member economies. It includes a database of current projects in this area with Internet links to most of them. Although most projects appearing in this database have indeed been initiated by member economies and are the responsibility of teams of participants from a subset of member economies, the ISTWG has had an important coordinating role. The series of technomarts (three have already been held, in Korea, Chinese Taipei, and Australia, and a fourth is under preparation) deserves special mention in regard to this coordinating role.

Actions Taken by Member Economies

As noted before, replies from four member economies were received in response to the questionnaire: Australia, Korea, Singapore, and Thailand, in addition to a reply from the APEC Secretariat.

Australia

Although the reply from Australia does not mention any initiatives arising from this member economy, the database in AST Web lists three ongoing projects initiated by Australia. One of them, already at the stage of trials and with the participation of Japan, Korea, Malaysia, Russia, and the United States, is the construction of a database of facilities and expertise in materials processing and testing. The other two projects deal respectively with earthquake simulation and the creation of a network to further collaboration on antibiotic resistance.

Korea

Korea has participated significantly in the technology areas of Environmental and Cleaner Production Strategies, Communications, Information Technologies/Electronics, and Sustainable Agriculture. In addition, Korea has three currently ongoing projects listed on the AST Web. One of them, co-sponsored by China, Japan, Hong Kong, and Singapore, is the International Molecular Biology Network (IMBN) for Asia and the Pacific Rim project. The project aims to promote biotechnology and biomedical research in the region.

Singapore

Singapore is the lead economy for the APEC Coordinating Centre for Good Clinical Practice (GCP) for the period 1996–2001, and it hosts the GCP Secretariat as well as drives the harmonization of GCP standards in APEC. On a second front, Singapore is a co-sponsor of the IMBN project (see above), and it hosts the IMBN Secretariat. Singapore also held the Second Youth Science Festival in July-August 2000.

Thailand

Its actions have been mostly in the area of improvement of information. It has two projects listed on the AST Web, one exploring the development of a post-harvest network for the APEC region, and the other is a study on megacities and technology and learning in 2010.

An examination of the AST Web database of projects, which contains fifty ongoing projects, reveals a concentration of projects among a few countries, especially Japan (main sponsor of fourteen projects), the USA (nine), and Chinese Taipei (eight). China and Canada sponsored three projects each, while Indonesia, Malaysia, and the Philippines sponsored one each.

Evaluation of Progress

Issue experts were asked to evaluate the progress in three areas, which were further subdivided into more detailed questions, as indicated below:

1. Networking and partnerships
   - 1.1 Exchange of technical and scientific information
   - 1.2 Participation in international scientific and technical projects
   - 1.3 Exchange of technical and scientific personnel
2. Business climate and participation
   - 2.1 Regulatory framework
   - 2.2 Relations between business and government
   - 2.3 Participation in international technological partnerships
3. Promotion of human resource development (HRD) activities that specifically relate to industrial science and technology.

Their replies are summarized in Table 1.

TABLE 1 **Evaluation of Progress**

	Australia	Korea	Singapore	Thailand	APEC
Networking & Partnership					
1.1	B	B	A	A	B
1.2	B	B	A	B	A
1.3	—	C	B	C	B
Business Climate					
2.1	B	A	C	C	C
2.2	B	B	B	B	C
2.3	B	B	B	B	B
HRD	B	B	A	B	A

Note: A = had significant impact
B = had minor impact
C = been irrelevant to the normal expected evolution

As might be expected, the evaluation gives higher marks to the achievements related to the exchange of technical and scientific information and participation in international projects. It also evaluates positively the advances related to human resource development activities. On the other hand, progress in the area of relations between business and government is judged to be mediocre, as also happens with participation in international technological partnerships, and with the exchange of technical and scientific personnel. The evaluation of advances related to the regulatory framework has mixed results, varying from significant to irrelevant, depending on the reporting country. Having a greater number of replies from issue experts would undoubtedly help in obtaining a better overall evaluation.

Assessment of Strengths and Weaknesses

The clarity of APEC commitments and the relatively strong government support are often given as positive points. Although some issue experts did not signal any weakness, a number of important negative points emerge from their replies.

- The lack of business interest in the science and technology process of APEC is signalled as a serious weakness;
- The limited capacity of the ISTWG to coordinate activities that often encompass the areas of interest of other working groups and fora hinders the efficacy of its action;
- The most serious weakness is related to the diversity of APEC membership. The wide gap in science and technology levels and stages of development limits wide and active participation by member economies. In particular, many of the projects identified are beyond the resources of member economies to participate and implement, not to mention their relevance to them;
- Lack of participation by universities; and
- Lack of resources to support participation by member economies and institutions.

Recommendations

The recommendations can be grouped under four headings: relations with business; better coordination; narrowing the focus; and resources.

Relations with Business

Ways must be found to deal with the lack of interest of business in the APEC process. The ISTWG should open its doors to the business sector and use its meetings as an opportunity to engage with them. In addition,

ABAC could be called upon to develop better links between industrial science and technology activities and enterprises in the region.

Better Coordination

APEC needs to restructure its organization to some extent, so as to better coordinate science and technology activities since these are initiated by different working groups.

Narrowing the Focus

There are too many projects on a large variety of subjects and it is unclear whether there is any structure at all in the projects. There is an inescapable perception that many of these initiatives are of an *ad hoc* nature. In addition, it is certainly unrealistic to expect progress in so many areas. It is highly recommended, therefore, to provide some focus and structure to the programme of activities. A simple way of approaching this objective would be to select one (or a limited number) of focal themes of activity for each year (or multi-year period). These themes would have to be selected in consultation with the member economies.

Resources

This is of course a difficult question, but it is of utmost importance to search for resources to stimulate the participation of less developed member economies. Cooperation in APEC needs to be highlighted.

9

ENERGY DEVELOPMENT IN APEC

John McKay

Given the current world-wide concern about the high price of oil, energy and the potential economic consequences of recent surges in the costs of fuel are bound to be dominant topics for discussion within various APEC fora in the immediate future. These are not new to APEC. Indeed, cooperation on energy issues has always been at the core of APEC's activities, and the Energy Working Group (EWG) of APEC can be regarded as one of the organization's most successful initiatives. It is a tribute to this past effort in the energy field that it seems unlikely that any change of direction will be necessary here: all the key questions raised by the current energy situation have been the subject of intensive work for a number of years. Indeed, the APEC Leaders' Statement from Brunei in November 2000 (Attachment 1, Paragraph 2) supported earlier statements from the APEC Energy Ministers, and re-emphasized the importance of efficient energy programmes for the future development of the region.

In the period just before the onset of the Asian financial crisis in 1997, when both growth rates and projections for future expansion were at their height, it was expected that regional demand for infrastructure, including the key element of power, would provide a massive challenge in the planning and implementation of investment. The World Bank

(1995), for example, estimated that in the period up to 2004 a total investment of US$1,587 billion would be needed in infrastructure in East Asia. This massive sum represents 6.6 per cent of total gross domestic product (GDP) in the region. Power constitutes one of the largest elements in this projected demand: investment needs in power are expected to be US$391 billion in East Asia, with a further US$115 billion in India. This represents 2 per cent of total GDP in East Asia. The greatest expansion is expected to be in China (US$150 billion), South Korea (US$80 billion), Indonesia (US$73 billion), and Thailand (US$38 billion).

The slowdown of economic activity, especially in the private sector, as a result of the Asian economic crisis, has given rise to some rapid reassessments in projected demands for power. This has been especially so in Southeast Asia. A report by the East Asia Analytical Unit of the Australian Department of Foreign Affairs and Trade (Australia 1998) has forecasted that in the major countries of Southeast Asia, electricity capacity growth would be halved in the period 1998–2001 (Table 1).

However, the more rapid than expected recovery from the crisis in a number of countries, plus the recognized role of infrastructure investment in generating renewed growth in the whole region has given rise to further reassessments of future demand.

Thus, energy is at the forefront of the debate about the future economic prospects of the region, and is an area which should be, and indeed has been, central to the activities of APEC. In this chapter, the contribution of APEC to energy development in the region will be outlined, together with some comments on possible future directions.

TABLE 1 **Electricity Capacity Growth Forecasts for Southeast Asia, 1998-2001**
(In gigawatts)

Country	Pre-Crisis Projections	Low Growth Scenario	High Growth Scenario
Indonesia	7.3	3.8	4.0
Malaysia	1.4	0.1	0.5
Philippines	3.6	2.8	3.3
Thailand	3.8	0.2	2.0
Total	16.1	6.9	9.8

SOURCE: Australia (1998), p.25.

Particular attention is given to the work of the EWG, which surely must be regarded as one of the real success stories of the APEC process. It is particularly useful, then, to identify some of the factors and approaches that have allowed the EWG to be so successful.

Summary of Key Initiatives

The basis for APEC's entire involvement in the energy field has been provided by the Osaka Action Agenda. While in some respects, the EWG is now moving beyond this 1995 agreement, the whole approach to energy set out there has been so basic that it is essential to outline this framework in some detail.

The Osaka Action Programme for Energy

The Action Programme for Energy that was agreed to in Osaka was based on the EWG's work programme up to that time, and incorporated the basic principles and goals produced by the EWG. Four basic goals were enunciated in the document:

1. Improving the understanding by governments and the business sectors of member economies of regional energy markets, thus assisting policy-making and business activities;
2. Reducing regulatory, institutional, and procedural impediments to trade and investment in energy infrastructure, products, and services;
3. Reducing the environmental impacts of energy production, delivery, and consumption through improving access to technology, training, services, and investment opportunities; and
4. Reducing costs to both governments and business by the acceptance of equivalence in accreditation and the closer harmonization of standards relating to energy products, appliances, and services.

At Bogor, the fourteen non-binding policy principles for rational energy consumption developed by the EWG were also endorsed. These fourteen principles, which are still central to the energy programme of APEC, are to:

1. emphasize the need to ensure that energy issues are addressed in a manner which gives full consideration to harmonization of economic development, security, and environmental factors;
2. pursue policies for enhancing the efficient production, distribution, and consumption of energy;
3. pursue open energy markets for achieving rational energy consumption, energy security, and environmental objectives, and

recommending action in the appropriate forum of APEC to remove impediments to the achievement of these ends;

4. recognize that measures to facilitate the rational consumption of energy might involve a mix of market-based and regulatory policies, with the relative components of the mix being a matter for the judgement of individual economies;
5. consider reducing energy subsidies progressively and promote implementation of pricing practices which reflect the economic cost of supplying and using energy across the full energy cycle, having regard to environmental costs;
6. regularly exchange experiences on the various policies being used by member economies to achieve more rational energy consumption.
7. ensure that a least costs approach to the provision of energy services is considered;
8. promote the adoption of policies to facilitate the transfer of efficient and environmentally sound energy technologies on a commercial and non-discriminatory basis;
9. encourage the establishment of arrangements for the development of human resource skills relevant to the application and operation of improved technology;
10. enhance energy information and management programmes to assist more rational energy decision-making;
11. encourage energy research, development, and demonstration to pave the way for cost-effective application of new, more efficient, and environmentally sound energy technologies;
12. promote capital flows through the progressive removal of impediments to the funding of the transfer and adoption of more energy efficient and environmentally sound technologies and infrastructure;
13. promote cost-effective measures which improve the efficiency with which energy is used but reduce greenhouse gases as part of a suggested regional response to greenhouse gas reductions; and
14. cooperate, to the extent consistent with each economy's development needs, in the joint implementation of projects to reduce greenhouse gas emissions consistent with the Climate Change Convention.

It should be noted that the energy goals and policy principles enunciated in Bogor address both elements of the APEC Action Agenda (trade and investment liberalization, and economic and technical cooperation).

At Bogor, the four basic goals already set out were further elaborated on, and a series of more specific initiatives were proposed:

1. *Fostering a Common Understanding of Regional Energy Issues*

Initiatives here included the consolidation of an energy database already started by the EWG, and the setting up of a collaborative regional energy outlook, to be produced with significant input from the private sector. The outlook aimed to foster member economies' understanding of the energy policy implications of future energy supply and demand trends, thus assisting decision-making processes.

A key element here was a proposal to establish an important research facility in the energy field. This was, in fact, set up in 1996 as the Asia-Pacific Research Centre (APERC), located in Japan and largely funded by the Japanese Government, but with some financial input from the EWG, and managed under the auspices of the EWG. The work of the APERC since 1996 will be reviewed later in this chapter, but it is relevant here to set out the major roles of APERC as envisaged in Bogor:

— a joint study on the compilation of the APEC regional energy outlook, and the development of a supporting research agenda.

— establishment of a "Know-How Transfer Programme" involving advisory missions, workshops, and training courses.

— establishment of an Energy Network, facilitating the electronic sharing of data, research results, and ideas on policy initiatives with a range of energy authorities.

2. *Facilitating Investment in the Energy Sector*

The activities proposed under this theme were designed to underpin regional economic growth by encouraging investment in various energy programmes. Work in this area was underpinned by the completion of an EWG study on the steps needed to facilitate private sector investment in energy infrastructure. The study argued that cooperative regional action could be very helpful in dealing with key issues and impediments, and individual economies would achieve more through regional cooperation than by acting alone. The study recommended that each member economy should focus on similarities in the issues faced, and also respect differences in the solutions adopted in particular circumstances; agreement of all member economies on specific work programmes should be sought; and intensive work activity should be carried out over short periods.

The study envisaged that well-developed regional cooperation would reduce business sector risk, and increase mutual understanding of alternative policy and regulatory approaches in various member economies. This, it was argued, would help in the design of more effective regulatory practices, lower the perception of risk in investing in the region, increase the transfer of technology and relevant skills, lower the cost of capital, facilitate regional trade in equipment and fuels, enhance energy security, and address environmental issues. The extent to which these themes have been developed since 1993 will be addressed later.

3. *Reducing Environmental Impacts in the Energy Sector*

The aim here was to reduce the environmental impacts of energy production, delivery and consumption through improving access to technology, training, services and investment opportunities. Two major strands were proposed in Bogor under this theme:

— *the facilitation of efficient and environmentally sound energy technologies.* Since fossil fuels dominate energy production in the region (oil 41 per cent, coal 31 per cent, natural gas 18 per cent, nuclear 7 per cent, and renewables 3 per cent) and are expected to continue in the immediate future, given that demand for energy is increasing, environmental impacts will increase. Thus, it is essential to ensure that technological and environmental advances are incorporated into new energy developments. The EWG had already, by 1995, undertaken programmes designed to address the various impediments to the uptake of environmentally sound technologies, increase knowledge of the relevant technologies available, develop the application of technologies to meet particular local circumstances, and assist in the efficient operation, and maintenance of these technologies. It was proposed that over the short and medium terms activities should aim to increase the adoption of cost-effective and environmentally sound technologies. Over the longer term, cooperative multilateral programmes to reduce climate change should be explored.

— *integrated demand-side management.* The EWG was requested to prepare a demand-side management manual for member economies, incorporating model programmes demonstrating the range of options available, and providing examples appropriate to different levels of economic development.

4. *Acceptance of Equivalence in Accreditation and Increasing Harmonization of Energy Standards*

It was argued that costs to both governments and business could be reduced if energy standards could be harmonized. Major immediate benefits would result from a harmonized network of protocols in member economies on basic product performance, methods of testing for determining energy consumption, and accreditation systems for laboratories and quality assurance systems and procedures. Moreover, significant trade and economic gains would arise from clarifying production and marketing requirements in all member economies, increasing certainty among market suppliers in terms of production planning, standardizing test protocols, and among regulators on accreditation procedures and quality assurance processes. It was noted that such work could only be successful if the private sector was closely involved. Liaison was also needed with the APEC Committee on Trade and Investment, which had begun work on the harmonization of standards for certain electrical and electronic products. Wider consultation may also be necessary with international bodies such as the International Energy Agency.

Energy Ministers' Meetings

Building upon the initiatives brought together in the Osaka Action Programme for Energy, four meetings of Energy Ministers have been held.

The first meeting was held in Sydney, Australia, in August 1996. The Ministers identified five objectives of fundamental importance to the region's future prosperity, and agreed to report these directly to APEC Economic Leaders. These challenges for cooperative action were:

1. *Energy security*. The level of energy self-sufficiency in the region varies widely, with some economies being large net exporters of energy, but the region as a whole is a net energy importer. The Ministers recognized the need for the APEC economies to cooperate more closely towards the development of the APEC energy community in a sustainable manner. This could be best achieved, it was agreed, by the actions of individual member economies and through cooperation to ensure the enhancement of an open, efficient regional energy market, diversity of the energy mix, and measures to achieve efficient energy production, distribution, and consumption. The role of high quality information and research in meeting these objectives was emphasized.
2. *Infrastructure investment*. The Ministers noted the high levels of investment needed to meet the greater demand for energy forecast at that time. Such investment was beyond the means of governments, and ways of involving the private sector had to be found. The work already done by the EWG on this issue was welcomed, including the major report on "Regional Cooperation for Power Infrastructure".

3. *Environment.* The Ministers agreed that an urgent priority was the application of economically sound measures to minimize the adverse environmental impacts of energy production and use in the region. Again, the initiatives already taken by the EWG in this area were endorsed. The Ministers agreed to cooperate in research and development, technology application and uptake, and programmes related to energy efficiency, clearer fuels, and renewable sources of energy.
4. *Reducing costs through cooperation on energy standards.* The Ministers noted that the application of product energy standards can provide a means for individual member economies to meet greater energy efficiency and improved environmental performances. It was agreed that an APEC multilateral framework can provide opportunities to overcome standards-related impediments to trade. The Ministers instructed officials from member economies to work together to achieve the benefits of increased cooperation on energy standards.
5. *Policy principles.* The Ministers agreed that their common goal should be to work towards the simultaneous achievement of economic growth, enhanced energy security, and mitigation of the impact of energy on the environment, by developing shared policy principles and enhancing closer cooperation. The Ministers considered and endorsed the fourteen non-binding energy policy principles agreed by the EWG and originally presented in Osaka (listed above).

The second Energy Ministers' meeting was held in Edmonton, Canada, in August 1997. The work of the EWG in advancing the issues discussed at the first meeting in Sydney was welcomed. The areas of basic concern identified in Sydney were again discussed and progress in each area was evaluated. Major new initiatives included:

1. *International Energy Business Symposium.* Ministers welcomed this initiative, and thanked participants for their report.
2. *Greenhouse Gases.* The meeting recognized the importance of accelerating action to deal with global emissions of greenhouse gases. The importance of the development of market opportunities related to the reduction of greenhouse gas emissions was also noted.
3. *Power Infrastructure.* The Ministers re-emphasized that power sector reform was an important element in meeting the region's growing power needs, and noted the important benefits of business sector participation in power infrastructure development. The Ministers endorsed the non-binding principles contained in the EWG's "Manual of Best Practice Principles for Independent Power Producers".
4. *Food, Energy, Environment, Economic Growth, and Population (FEEEP).* The Ministers discussed ways in which the work of the EWG could

enhance moves towards a more sustainable and prosperous future. The Ministers thanked Canada for its efforts in organizing a symposium on the complex issues contained in the FEEEP agenda.

The third meeting, held in Okinawa, Japan, in October 1998 reflected the new mood after the Asian crisis. Taking as their theme "Energy: Driving Force for Economic Recovery and Development", the Ministers discussed the serious economic plight of a number of APEC members, and the implications for the energy sector. The importance of implementing the fourteen non-binding energy policy principles in the current situation was strongly supported. It was argued that open and efficient energy markets could play a key role in stimulating recovery. Within this new context, the Ministers reviewed some of the key elements of the programmes that had been agreed at earlier meetings:

1. *Energy Security.* In spite of the downturn in economic growth, demand was still expected to outpace energy production by a wide margin. There was a real danger that in the new situation, investment would be curtailed. Supply diversification, energy efficiency, and infrastructure development would become even more important. The EWG initiative to share information on oil markets and to discuss oil supply and demand security issues was strongly endorsed.
2. *Energy Infrastructure.* The Ministers recognized that continuous development of adequate energy infrastructure was essential as a stimulus for economic recovery, as well as for sustainable development in the region. In the current situation, the need to enhance private sector confidence in energy investments in the region was paramount. To this end, the EWG was asked to hold a business/government workshop to discuss this issue and develop recommendations.
3. *Natural Gas Initiative.* Meeting expected demand for energy over the next twenty years will require increased natural gas production and significant new infrastructure development. The Asian Development Bank has estimated that as much as US$70 billion will be needed in investment in new natural gas infrastructure in Asia over the next fifteen years. The Ministers agreed that a new APEC Natural Gas Initiative was needed to promote the acceleration of investment in natural gas supplies, infrastructure, and trading networks in the region. Feasibility studies on pipeline projects in the region should be conducted.
4. *Energy Efficiency.* The EWG was instructed to develop a programme to exchange information on policies, technologies, and practices to improve the efficient production, transportation, and consumption of energy.

The fourth meeting held in San Diego, USA, in May 2000 represented an important new direction, with the emphasis now being placed on the implementation of the policies, research recommendations, and practical suggestions put forward during the previous decade. The theme was "Turning Vision into Reality", and the Ministers committed to the implementation of energy initiatives on a voluntary basis, and endorsed a new implementation strategy. The Ministers agreed that the time was now ripe to turn all this earlier work into reality. Many of the economies are undergoing energy sector reform and stand to benefit from the shared experience of other economies in coping with the transition to more open, competitive markets. Moreover, rising demand and the resultant dependence on oil supplies from outside the region have made energy security a major concern. Under the new implementation strategy, invited teams would visit economies to share experiences on initiatives and agreed principles. A system of self-reporting on a voluntary basis by members involved in implementation programmes would be instituted, with the whole strategy being re-evaluated after three years. Requests for an implementation facilitation team visit are made to the Chair of the EWG. This new programme has already been initiated, with Thailand requesting the team visit. A report on this new initiative will be presented later.

Actions Taken at the International Level

The narrative presented in the earlier section has attempted to portray the gradual and incremental development of the APEC approach to energy. The emphasis has been on the accumulation of data and research findings, carefully staged agreement on policy principles, the involvement of the private sector in the whole process, and finally the development of an agreed implementation strategy. All of this has been made possible by the development of an effective infrastructure, spearheaded by the EWG. In this section, the structure and work of the EWG and a number of related groups will be outlined. Between them, these organizations have produced a massive amount of research, and it is only possible here to give a brief outline of these rich sources of material.

The Energy Working Group

The EWG was established in 1990, and to date has held twenty meetings, the latest being in Cusco, Peru, in October 2000. Its role is to help maximize the energy sector's contribution to the region's economic and social well-being, and to achieve this goal, four objectives have been set out:

1. Fostering a common understanding of regional energy issues;
2. Facilitating trade and investment in the energy sector;

3. Reducing the environmental impact of the energy sector; and
4. Accepting equivalence in accreditation and harmonization of energy standards.

Each of these objectives has been set out in the EWG's Operational Plan revised in 2000, identifying strategies to achieve the agreed objectives. For each objective a set of outcomes, benefits, beneficiaries, activities, outputs, and performance indicators has been outlined.

The EWG is assisted in its work by five expert groups (as of 2001, there have been some minor name changes, but the original titles are used here):

1. *The Expert Group on Energy Data and Analysis.* This group is responsible for carrying out work under the energy supply and demand theme. It has worked on establishing a consistent framework for energy data reporting and forecasting for the APEC region. The group publishes an annual energy data time series with a common data format for the region. It is also responsible for the oversight of the Asia-Pacific Energy Research Centre (APERC), which is discussed below.
2. *The Expert Group on Clean Fossil Energy.* This group is responsible for the energy and the environment theme. Its role is to enhance economic development and mitigate at a local, regional, and global level all environmental impacts related to the production, preparation, transport, storage, and use of fossil fuels and their derivatives.
3. *The Expert Group on Energy Efficiency and Conservation.* This group is responsible for work under the energy efficiency and conservation programme. Initiatives have concentrated on encouraging the adoption of policies and programmes to promote energy conservation and the application of energy-efficient technologies.
4. *The Expert Group on New and Renewable Energy Technologies.* This group is responsible for work under the energy research, development, and technology transfer theme. Initiatives here have focused on maximizing the degree of new and renewable technology assimilation by member economies by increasing their ability to assess, operate, maintain, and adapt both existing and new technologies.
5. *The Expert Group on Minerals and Energy Exploration and Development (EGMEED).* EGMEED is responsible for work under the energy exploration and development theme. The group seeks to promote issues relating to minerals and energy exploration within APEC, including the gathering and distribution of information regarding minerals and energy exploration and development, and market demand.

The EWG and its expert groups have published a wide range of detailed and high-quality publications. These include:

- a regular newsletter, *Energy Matters: Newsletter of the APEC Energy Working Group;*
- *Coal and Natural Gas Competition in APEC Economies* (1999);
- *Institutionalisation of a Benchmarking System for Data on Energy Use in Commercial and Industrial Buildings* (1999);
- *APEC Energy Demand and Supply Outlook* (1998);
- *Promoting Energy Security in APEC through Improved International Fuel Market Operations* (1998);
- *APEC Manual of Best Practice Principles for Independent Power Producers* (1997);
- *Environmentally Sound Infrastructure in APEC Electricity Sectors* (1997);
- *Development of Analytic Methodologies to Incorporate Renewable Energy in Domestic Energy Planning* (1999);
- *APEC Energy Statistics* (regular series since 1992);
- *APEC Historical Energy Statistics 1980–1992* (1994);
- *Developing Transparent, Efficient, and Effective Procurement Processes for Power Infrastructure in APEC Member Economies* (1997);
- *APEC Energy R & D Technology Transfer and Renewable Energy Resource Assessment* (1996);
- *Directory of Demand Side Management* (1995).

The most recent publication of the EWG deserves special mention. *Trade and Investment Liberalisation in APEC: Economic and Energy Sector Impacts* (2000), produced for the EWG by the Australian Bureau of Agricultural and Resource Economies (ABARE), models the economic impacts of the trade and investment liberalization programme of APEC and then draws out the implications for the energy sector. This is done on a regional and country basis.

Asia Pacific Energy Research Centre

APERC was established in 1996 in Tokyo as an affiliated body of the Institute of Energy Economics, Japan. It is guided by the APEC Energy Working Group on Regional Energy Cooperation through the Expert Group on Energy Data and Outlook. Its research is undertaken by researchers from APEC member economies under a system of research fellowships. The primary objective of APERC is to foster understanding of future energy supply and demand trends and associated energy policy implications, which is in turn designed to improve the quality of available energy information, and therefore the efficiency of regional energy markets. In 1997, APERC produced a long-term energy demand/supply outlook for the region extending to 2010. Currently, the centre is undertaking research on six themes:

1. energy pricing practices and their implications for energy efficiency, the environment and supply infrastructure;
2. energy efficiency indicators for industry;
3. costs and benefits of a large-scale development of natural gas resources;
4. a feasibility study of a regional power interconnection network in the region;
5. deregulation and privatization of the electricity sector in the APEC economies;
6. the value of oil stocks for the security of oil supplies.

A number of research reports have been published on each of these themes.

EWG Business Network

In the summary of the four meetings of the Energy Ministers, frequent mention was made of the role of the private sector. Business sector input to the work of the EWG is done by the EWG Business Network, which was established to provide a business perspective on energy-related issues that can be considered through the APEC process. Each member economy can nominate a maximum of two representatives to the Energy Business Network (EBN). The PECC Energy Forum (discussed below) is represented on the EBN as an observer. The EBN has so far held three meetings: in Oakland, California; in Wellington, New Zealand; and in Melbourne, Australia. Representation is at a very high level, including the chief executives of some of the largest energy companies in the region.

APEC Energy Regulators' Forum

This forum provides a regular meeting place for energy regulators from around the region to exchange information and learn from the experience of other economies. So far, seven meetings have been held, the most recent in Brunei in April 2000. The Forum publishes summaries of regulatory arrangements in the APEC member economies in areas such as electricity regulation, gas regulation, power sector regulation, tariff pricing policies, and power purchase arrangements.

PECC Energy Forum

The PECC Energy Forum is the task force of the Pacific Economic Cooperation Council (PECC) that brings together energy business leaders, policy-makers, and researchers to address critical issues of energy supply, demand, security, and policy in the region. The group is represented at the APEC Energy Ministers and their senior officials meetings. The private sector is very much in the lead in this forum. Three business meetings have been held in conjunction with the meetings of Energy Ministers. A series of publications have been prepared, the most recent being *Natural Gas in Asia: Facts and Fiction*.

APEC Public/Private Sector Dialogue on Infrastructure

APEC has convened a series of public/private sector dialogues on infrastructure, the latest being in Melbourne in December 2000, organized by the Australian APEC Study Centre. While these dialogues cover the whole area of infrastructure development, with particular emphasis being given to public/private sector cooperation in areas such as finance, there is much attention given to the particular needs of the energy sector. More general topics that have relevance to energy are also discussed — for example, questions of privatization, regulation, and the protection of shareholder interests. A more detailed analysis of this dialogue process is presented in the chapter on infrastructure in this volume.

Actions Taken at the Level of Member Economies

Throughout the region, there has been a movement towards more competitive markets in energy, and in many economies energy organizations have been privatized. In no small measure, this is probably due to the work of the EWG over the last decade. Incrementally, policy-makers have been drawn into discussions about the kinds of energy policies agreed by APEC, and the private sector has also been heavily involved. However, this section will focus on the latest development in the work of the EWG: the implementation strategy designed to assist individual member economies, discussed earlier in this report.

As already stated, the basis of this approach is the Implementation Facilitation Assistance Team (IFAT) programme, under which, at the request of a member economy, the EWG will put together a team of energy experts to visit the host economy to share experiences and provide advice on options and approaches to implementing energy market reform. Team members are drawn from a cross-section of APEC economies, including representatives of the EWG Business Network, the Energy Regulators' Forum, and other nominated experts. The approach was pioneered in November 1999 when the Royal Thai Government invited a team of experts to Thailand to discuss natural gas reforms. A follow-up visit was made in August 2000 to develop and discuss specific recommendations. Thailand and the IFAT members considered the process to be extremely helpful and constructive. In particular, it assisted government representatives:

— to develop an energy market reform process which suited their specific needs;
— to obtain advice from experts from within APEC who have gone through, or are going through, similar reform processes; and
— to come together with parties who would not otherwise meet, to discuss relevant issues in an informal forum.

For business participants, the IFAT process provides an opportunity:

— to discuss relevant market reform issues from a business perspective;
— to obtain information on energy markets within the APEC region; and
— to look for possible investment opportunities, and to establish high-level contacts.

Both Peru and the Philippines have advised that they will be inviting IFAT visits in the near future, and the United States has indicated that it will invite an IFAT team on electricity markets during 2001. Other invitations are likely to follow.

Evaluation

Evaluation of APEC's work in energy is based on three sources: the return of two completed questionnaires, one from Chile and one from Thailand; detailed discussions with staff from the EWG, based in Canberra; and my own detailed reading of the mass of documents put out by the EWG.

Questionnaire Responses

Chile

This respondent rated the output of the EWG very highly. The *APEC Energy Statistics* and the *Regional Energy Supply and Demand Outlook* were both regarded as very useful, allowing Chile to see the context of its own development. The expert groups are also seen as making very useful contributions. In Chile's case, EGMEED was rated particularly relevant. The environmental group has also developed a very useful programme, allowing discussion of environmental impact mitigation and prevention.

Thailand

Thailand has been heavily involved in EWG activities, and is extremely supportive of them. The fourteen non-binding policy principles have already been endorsed as a Cabinet Resolution of the Royal Thai Government. The environmental concerns explored by the EWG are extremely important. Training courses and seminars have been very useful, and are an effective way to bring about mutual benefits to the APEC economies. The publication, *Regional Energy Supply and Demand Outlook*, is regarded as very useful in energy planning. The expert groups were rated highly, especially the expert group on Clean Fossil Fuel and the Expert Group on New and Renewable Energy Technologies. The Energy Business Network has made substantial contributions, as has the meeting of Energy Ministers. The response suggested two areas of improvements. Energy statistics are sometimes a little out of date, and the use of electronic networks might overcome this. In addition, more detailed "how to" practical sessions could be more widely utilized.

EWG Self-Evaluation

Members of the EWG secretariat itself generally rate the activities of the group very highly, and believe that the strategies developed have been the correct ones. They argue that this success has been based on several factors:

— continuity of the Chair. Australia has chaired the EWG from the very beginning, and this provides the important advantages of continuity;
— the staff of the EWG secretariat is adequate, with three full-time members funded by the Australian Government;
— the funding given by the Japanese Government to the APERC has provided an essential research base for the activities of the EWG; and
— continuity in the APEC Secretariat has also been vital, with Mr. Yang Yafei playing a very constructive role over many years.

Involvement by individual member economies is variable, but most have been very supportive. The EWG at present has a number of guest members from non-APEC economies. Currently, India, Pakistan, Colombia, Venezuela, Bangladesh, and Mongolia are members, but again with varying degrees of involvement.

My Evaluation

One cannot but be impressed by the range of activities organized by APEC in the energy sector. Publications and research are extremely detailed and focused, and are of the highest quality. The participation of the private sector is now at a very high level. I rate this performance as excellent.

Recommendations

Given the importance of energy to the future of the region, and especially in the light of current concerns about energy security, it is imperative that the EWG continues its work. Research, seminars, and publications are all needed in a range of areas. The proposal by the EWG to provide more up-to-date information via its website is strongly supported. Assistance in deregulating energy production and distribution is needed in many economies, and hence the new facilitation programme is very welcome.

References

Australia. *Asia's Infrastructure in the Crisis: Harnessing Private Enterprise.* Canberra: East Asia Analytical Unit, Department of Foreign Affairs and Trade, 1988.

Australia. *Trade and Investment Liberalisation in APEC: Economic and Energy Sector Impacts.* Canberra: Australian Bureau of Agricultural and Resource Economics & APEC Energy Working Group, 2000.

World Bank. *Infrastructure Development in Asia and the Pacific: Towards a New Public-Private Partnership.* Washington DC: World Bank, 1995.

10

DEVELOPMENT OF ECONOMIC INFRASTRUCTURE

JOHN MCKAY

In the period leading up to the onset of the Asian economic crisis in 1997, when it was confidently expected that high growth rates would continue uninterrupted for many years, it was forecast that demand for investment in infrastructure would provide a massive challenge for the region. The World Bank (1995) estimated that in the period up to 2004, a total investment of US$1,587 billion would be needed in infrastructure as a whole in East Asia. This represented 6.6 per cent of total gross domestic product (GDP) in the region. It was expected that in East Asia some US$211 billion would be needed for telecommunications, US$391 billion for power, US$528 billion for transport, and US$132 billion for water and sanitation. The slowdown in economic activity, especially in the private sector, as a result of the crisis, has given rise to some reassessment of these needs, especially in Southeast Asia (Australia 1998). However, the more rapid than expected recovery since 1997 in a number of countries, plus the recognized role of infrastructural investment in generating renewed growth in the whole region, has ensured that the question of economic infrastructure is still a priority area in the region.

The question of energy, obviously a key component here, has been addressed in a separate chapter, so here I will concentrate on other aspects of infrastructure, and on the role that APEC has played and can be expected to play in the future. It will be argued that the infrastructure question is not just about building roads and bridges, but about the design and construction of a complex, ongoing system. Thus, issues such as human resources and management skills are crucial, and this suggests a broader role for APEC.

Summary of Key Initiatives

The general theme of infrastructure cuts across the agendas of a range of APEC working groups and other fora, but since 1999 there has been an effort to draw together the whole picture and understand the linkages between various areas. Before the crisis, the attention within APEC on infrastructure issues was dominated by concern for two problem areas. The first involved the ways in which sufficient funds could be assembled to meet the expected infrastructural needs of the region. This theme was concerned with the perceptions and needs of the private sector, interactions with governments, and the creation of an appropriate regulatory environment to encourage investment. Secondly, there was concern with the supply of a sufficient number of trained people to manage, build, maintain, and run the many large-scale projects that were expected to be needed. Since then, these issues have remained relevant, but there has also been a need to consider the role that infrastructural development can play in stimulating regional recovery. Each of these themes is considered below.

Provision of Investment Finance

Discussions within APEC have been based on the assumption that infrastructure is absolutely vital to the future of the region. Good infrastructure is essential for the competitiveness of an economy, while poor services in this area can seriously impede growth and productivity. However, from the point of view of investors, infrastructure projects have a series of special characteristics. In many cases, they:

- are large and elaborate;
- have a long life and hence a long investment payback period;
- enjoy large economies of scale;
- have very large sunk costs;
- involve lumpy investments;
- provide "essential" services;
- have networked delivery systems; and
- are a public good, with neither rival nor excludable consumption features.

Increasingly, attention has turned to the ways in which the private sector can be involved in the financing of such projects, bearing in mind these special characteristics, and also in the ownership and management of these projects, either through the privatization of existing facilities, or the construction of new projects. Lynch (1996) has reviewed alternative funding mechanisms that can be employed by governments, including:

- finance from government consolidated revenue or borrowings;
- overseas aid, for developing countries;
- borrowing through specialized banks or agencies (for example, the Japanese long-term credit banks); and
- borrowing from domestic capital markets (for example, long-term infrastructure bonds).

Such mechanisms can provide governments with the funds they need, but the repayment is not dependent on the success of the project, and the lenders do not absorb any project risk, with government guarantees providing security for the investment. The involvement of the private sector in the process opens up a new set of funding mechanisms, including:

- participant capital injections;
- bank finance (for example, through syndicated loans);
- debt issues on domestic capital markets;
- sale of equity rights in the project; and
- borrowing on international capital markets.

Here, repayment of borrowings is often partly dependent on the success of the project, although some governments may seek to attract investment by offering revenue flows, or sales guarantees. After reviewing the advantages and problems of private sector involvement in various stages of a project — planning, design, construction, operation, maintenance, ownership, etc. — Lynch suggests that we may like to see as the preferred model some variant of the build-own-operate-transfer (BOOT) arrangement. Indeed, within APEC there has been considerable discussion of this system and how it can be made more effective.

There remains, of course, a crucial role for government in the regulation of infrastructure systems, including the supervision of appropriate service levels and pricing. Again, APEC has been much concerned with sharing experience in the area of regulation and helping member economies design more effective systems of their own. Particular regulation problems exist in sectors being transferred from public to private ownership, and these have received special attention.

Provision of Skilled Personnel

Given the sheer scale of projected demand for new facilities, grave doubts have been expressed about the availability of a sufficient number of trained personnel in engineering, management, and other areas. APEC has become involved in this area in several ways. The Human Resource Development Working Group has been working on ways of allowing easier movement of trained engineers throughout the region by streamlining the system of recognition of qualifications. Another initiative, supported financially by the Government of Australia, has involved the holding of a series of workshops and training programmes, provided by the Australian APEC Study Centre. The first of these, held in Melbourne in 1997, brought together staff from Indonesia, Thailand, and the Philippines. The programme addressed the need for officials to improve existing skill levels in areas such as costing and delivering services and managing financial resources, and the need to develop new skills appropriate to the demands of privatization — such as risk assessment, competitiveness principles, and the development of new regimes of regulation. It was recognized that skill demands will vary from country to country, and participants were required to evaluate the particular needs and skill shortages in their own situations, and to place these demands within the key priority areas of infrastructure in their economy.

After the Crisis

At the Sixth APEC Finance Ministers Meeting in Langkawi, Malaysia, in May 1999, the Ministers agreed that revitalizing infrastructure development was a key component of regional recovery. In particular, it was recognized that the financing of infrastructure poses an important challenge, especially in the post-crisis financial environment. The Ministers noted that while the crisis had affected the demand for new investment in the region, the need for new projects was still very large, ensuring the continued need for substantial private sector involvement. The Ministers discussed a report by the Asian Development Bank (ADB) on "Private Sector Participation and Infrastructure Investment in Asia: The Impact of the Crisis", and supported a series of recommendations put forward there, notably:

- the need for governments to concentrate on planning, policy and regulation, and to involve the private sector in the development and operation of infrastructure facilities;
- the advantages of "unbundling" infrastructure services and introducing competition;
- the urgency of accelerating the development of domestic capital markets and, in particular, bond markets, to avoid currency and maturity mismatches in the future.

- The need to introduce independent, transparent, and consistent legal and regulatory regimes.

APEC's more specific work on infrastructure since the crisis has mainly been the responsibility of the Infrastructure Workshop (IWS), a sub-forum operating under the auspices of the Economic Committee. However, as a result of the 1999 Management Review, it was agreed that the IWS should be reconstituted as an *ad hoc* forum under the Ecotech Sub-Committee. An Action Programme for Infrastructure Development was launched in 1996, before the onset of the crisis, to provide the basis for APEC work on infrastructure. Joint activities under the Action Programme include analytical work on a wide range of infrastructure issues, implementation of programmes of information-sharing and training to enhance the environment for infrastructure improvement, and the conduct of public–private sector dialogues. An "infrastructure best practices" brochure was issued in 1996 to guide government officials, investors, developers, and lenders. The current activities of the IWS are discussed in the next section.

Actions Taken at the International Level

As was noted in the previous section, the APEC initiatives on economic infrastructure are mainly organized through the IWS. Its current and recent activities include:

- A series of public/private sector dialogues, beginning with the 1999 Public Business/Private Sector Dialogue on Infrastructure and Sustainable Development held in Kuala Terengganu, Malaysia. The sub-themes of this dialogue were "Sustainable Urbanization for the 21st Century", and "Preparing Investment for the Information Age and Beyond".
- The Regional Integration for Sustainable Economies (RISE) initiative, coordinated by the United States. This aims to develop an approach to rural development based on integrating rural economies into the broader market-place to increase efficiency and provide the basis for structural adjustment.
- The Infrastructure for Sustainable Cities initiative coordinated by Canada and Malaysia. This focuses on capacity building and information support for policy-makers.
- The development of the APEC Infrastructure Facilitation Network (AIFN), designed to encourage the evolution of facilitation networks of infrastructure agencies. Related to this, Chinese Taipei is facilitating the continued participation of the private sector in a network of APEC Infrastructure Resource Integration Centres linking region-wide groups involved in infrastructure development.

- An Economic Regulation and Creditworthiness Enhancement Programme is currently being conducted as a domestically oriented work team by Indonesia with support from Canada, the United States, the World Bank, and the ADB. It involves the application of best practice approaches identified in previous infrastructure dialogues through a roundtable involving stakeholders and experts.
- The 1999 Infrastructure Workshop undertook analytical work on the impact of the crisis on infrastructure demand, supply, and government policies. Its main project, on regional integration for sustainable economies, highlighted the importance of having the right infrastructure in place to support economic development, a key issue for economies emerging from the crisis.

The latest public/private sector dialogue, held in Melbourne in late 2000, gives an indication of the strength and usefulness of the process. The programme began with a consideration of the global and regional challenges facing the sector, and included input from the World Bank as well as from individual member economies. However, the major part of the dialogue was concerned with problems in designing regulatory frameworks in the new era, which would encourage investment while protecting consumers. A series of presentations highlighted the problems from a government perspective, and this was followed by inputs for a number of investors. Issues in competition policy, funding, risk management, and ownership were explored in detail. Finally, barriers to growth, capacity-building needs and ways of mapping progress in a changing environment were analysed.

A number of other APEC working groups are also involved in more specific infrastructure activities. The Transportation Working Group was created to foster economic development in the region through recommendations to increase the efficiency of the regional transportation system. Since it was formed in 1991, the Group has held nine Working Group meetings, and a Ministerial Meeting in 1995. The Telecommunications Working Group has been charged with the development of an Asia-Pacific Information Infrastructure, which will promote policy and regulatory measures to liberalize trade and investment in the region's telecommunications and information sector. The Group, established in 1990, has held a large number of meetings and joint activities. However, the activities in transport and telecommunications are both large topics in their own right and are not explored here.

Actions Taken at the Level of Member Economies

As has been noted, the involvement of APEC in the development of infrastructure has not been at the level of planning or financing of individual projects. Rather, the emphasis has been at the conceptual level — sharing experiences, learning from successful approaches, avoiding mistakes made by others — and in encouraging dialogue between various interest groups in the area, such as investors, planners, regulators. Given the loose nature of APEC, this is perhaps the most that could be expected. However, this makes it practically impossible to evaluate the precise impacts of the process in individual economies. Participants in the training programme held in Melbourne in 1997 were very enthusiastic about the value of such an event. It allowed them space to evaluate their own experience, analyse the needs of their own situation, and learn from others. One hopes that this improved their practice when they returned home, but it is difficult to be sure, or to measure the impact. Similarly, the public/private sector dialogue on infrastructure held in Melbourne in 2000 produced good interaction between various interested parties, but it is premature to assess whether this will result in new projects, or improved regulation. All that one can say is that participants found such things useful and would attend the next event. Given the size of the problem, and the immense efforts needed to transform existing systems and create new ones, such a process is a useful and productive step.

Evaluation and Recommendations

No completed questionnaire was received by the author, and thus the evaluation was based on the output from the APEC Group on Economic Infrastructure, and from attendance at the public/private sector dialogue in Melbourne. My view, as was noted above, is that the steps taken so far have been useful and should continue. Certainly, this is the intention of the IWS, and a number of commentators have expressed support for the emerging process. Andrew Elek (2000), for example, has argued that:

> APEC is finding a niche in helping to sustain adequate investment in the region's economic infrastructure, including for transport and communications. It is now widely accepted that the bulk of such investment will need to be financed by the private sector. ECOTECH can help gather and disseminate information on best practices on matters ranging from transparent tendering procedures to options for sharing risks between investors and users (Elek 2000, p. 30).

However, in order to satisfy the demands of the various interested parties, it will probably be necessary to move beyond the simple exchange of experiences. The IWS itself is proposing a review of relevant work in other APEC fora, such as sustainable urban development, to assess the future role of APEC in a more integrated approach to the field. This is an important step that should be taken with some urgency, given the importance of infrastructure to the future of the region.

References

Australia. *Asia's Infrastructure in the Crisis: Harnessing Private Enterprise.* Canberra: East Asia Analytical Unit, Department of Foreign Affairs and Trade, 1998.

Elek, Andrew. *Capacity Building in the Asia Pacific: A Way Forward for ECOTECH.* Brisbane: Foundation for Development Cooperation, 2000.

Lynch, David. *Financing Private Infrastructure Projects: Australian Investment Banks' Experience.* Issues Paper No. 8. Melbourne: Australian APEC Study Centre, 1996.

World Bank. *Infrastructure Development in Asia and the Pacific: Towards a New Public-Private Partnership.* Washington DC: World Bank, 1995.

_____. *Frontiers of the Public-Private Interface in East Asia's Infrastructure.* Washington DC: World Bank, 1996.

11

THE REFORM OF CORPORATE GOVERNANCE AFTER THE ASIAN ECONOMIC CRISIS

JOHN MCKAY

Defining the Problem

In the large and still growing literature on the Asian economic crisis and its aftermath, corporate governance has been identified by a number of commentators as a key issue. In perhaps the most strident analysis, Michael Backman (1999) has identified dubious business practices as a key contributor to the crisis:

> An Asian corporation can be compared to a kingdom — both are run autocratically and each has its ruling family. In essence, the Confucian precept that there is just one source of indivisible power means that Asian companies don't take well to notions of checks and balances, accountability, transparency, and good corporate governance. The demand for corporate transparency, for example, carries with it the implication that the controlling family might not be behaving as it should. Yielding to such demands means acknowledging other sources of power and hence a loss of authority. Similarly, the sharing of power with formal rules is eschewed.... Outsiders

> are precisely that and are dealt with via strategems and subterfuge. And the most anonymous of outsiders — minority shareholders in listed companies are treated the most derisorily of all. They, by definition, have no personal relationship with the controlling shareholder and are treated accordingly. (Backman 1999, p. 21.)

Similarly, Stephen Vines (1999), in a chapter on "Asian Corporate Myths", suggests that the crisis was really a crisis of management, a crisis of the way business is conducted in Asia. Kotler and Kartajaya (2000) strongly argue that new forms of corporate governance are essential in the repositioning of Asia that is now taking place.

There are, of course, many alternative definitions of the term "corporate governance". After a detailed review of the literature, On Kit Tam (1999) suggests that most definitions have been based on the Anglo-American corporate environment with its traditional issues and concerns, and for the current environment in Asia a more general notion of corporate governance is needed. With this in mind, he proposes that the term means "the processes and mechanisms for ensuring that a company performs in a responsible, responsive and pro-active way in the interests of its stakeholders" (p.18). Following a very detailed analysis of macroeconomic and financial sector linkages in the crisis, Alba et al. (1999) suggest that four aspects of corporate governance were critical in generating the problems of 1997:

— concentrated ownership;
— weak market incentives;
— protecting minority shareholders; and
— poor accounting standards and practices.

These areas are, of course, partly about issues of regulation, competition policy, and of government control and supervision, but also include questions of the behaviour, culture, and transparency of the corporation itself. It is this interface between public policy and the corporation itself which lends this important question amenable to actions from organizations such as APEC. However, this is also a very difficult area for APEC. Given the clear differences in business culture between the West and many parts of Asia, the advanced economies can leave themselves open to charges of arrogance or tunnel vision if they argue for a convergence in corporate governance practices. Certainly, many commentators would argue that such systems can only change slowly, since they are deeply embedded in the national culture and system of operations. Haggard (2000) has noted that relationships between government and business have followed a distinctive pattern in the development of the Asian "miracle", but any thorough reform of corporate governance will require a redefinition of this relationship, which will not be easy. Some Asian writers have, in my view, seriously underestimated the problem of such reform. Hoon et al.(2000) even suggest that "the family oriented approach to management, prevalent in many Asian, and particularly Chinese businesses, will need to be changed so that modern management practices and structures can be implemented" (p.11). The reality, I suspect, will not be easy even if one can be convinced that it is desirable.

Summary of Key Initiatives

APEC initiatives in the reform of corporate governance are obviously quite new, essentially since the Asian crisis. Thus, these initiatives have been largely in the areas of problem formulation, statements of basic principles and policies, and the collection of data. Many of the initiatives started have not yet been completed. Hence, this is very much in the nature of a progress report on a new programme.

Improvements in corporate governance were recognized as a key area of concern in generating recovery from the crisis at both meetings of Leaders in Vancouver and in Kuala Lumpur. However, more detailed proposals and initiatives came forward in 1999. At the Sixth APEC Finance Ministers Meeting in Langkawi, Malaysia, discussions were held with the Managing Director of the International Monetary Fund (IMF), the President of the World Bank, and the President of the Asian Development Bank (ADB) on the economic and financial situation in the region and on the best strategies for ensuring long-term growth. Attention was directed to the development of capital markets, and corporate governance was given special mention here. The Ministers gave high priority to domestic reform measures and endorsed the recommendations of a report on "Strengthening Corporate Governance in the APEC Region". The Ministers also recommended that member economies should take note of the findings of an OECD (Organization for Economic Cooperation and Development) task force on the principles of corporate governance. Member economies were asked to report, on a voluntary basis, on measures they were taking to improve corporate governance at the next Ministerial Meeting. The Ministers also supported the development of training programmes to improve the skills of accountants, auditors, company directors, regulators, and in the judicial system. The initiative of Australia in providing a compendium on its corporate governance training facilities was welcomed, and participants from the region were encouraged to take advantage of these possibilities. Members were urged to strengthen, where relevant, the quality of auditing and accounting standards, and to move towards standards that meet or exceed international norms. It was also agreed that insolvency law reforms were particularly important in the speedy restructuring of the business and financial sectors. A joint APEC-OECD workshop on insolvency law to be hosted by Australia later that year was welcomed. In the longer term, the meeting stressed the need for strengthening financial systems, regulation of key areas, and enhancing transparency and disclosure standards. The establishment of an APEC Core Group on Corporate Governance, led by Malaysia, in collaboration with Australia, the United States, the World Bank, and the ADB was welcomed. The initiative of Australia in hosting a symposium on corporate governance in November 1998 was applauded (a more detailed report on this initiative is given below). The role of credit-rating agencies in developing capital markets in the region and in strengthening disclosure standards was also discussed. Improvements in banking supervision procedures were also recognized as being important. These ideas were taken a stage further in May 1999 in a report to APEC Finance Ministers, partly based on studies by consultants of the Asian Development Bank and the World Bank. This report is also outlined in more detail below.

At the Seventh APEC Finance Ministers' Meeting in Brunei in September 2000, corporate governance issues again received some attention. It was argued that sound corporate governance was in part needed to encourage the return of capital to the region. To aid this process, it was announced that APEC would host a policy dialogue on strengthening corporate governance in early 2001. Indonesia has also offered to host a conference on insolvency law, as a follow-up to the 1999 meeting in Australia, in early 2001. A task force was also formed to report on company accounting and financial reporting in the region. The APEC fora on privatization, pension fund reform, and public sector management, held since the last Ministerial Meeting, were welcomed. Links to a range of OECD fora, such as the OECD Privatization Network, were noted. The contentious issue of credit-rating agencies was discussed, and it was announced that a special forum would be held in Manila in late 2000 to discuss a survey of agencies in the region. The Ministers also welcomed the establishment of a series of targeted symposiums and training programmes, organized by the Australian APEC Study Centre, aimed at the improved regulation of life insurance and pension industries in Asia.

Actions Taken at the International Level

As was noted above, most of the initiatives in this area are still in the early stages of implementation, but some progress can be reported.

Symposium in Australia

A special symposium was held in Sydney, Australia, on 1–3 November 1998 on "Corporate Governance in APEC: Rebuilding Asian Growth".

This was funded by the Australian Agency for International Development, and supported also by the Treasury of Australia, and managed by the Australian APEC Study Centre. It brought together key corporate leaders from around the region, representatives of international organizations, and government representatives. Reported below is a summary of the major findings and recommendations of the symposium. Since this seminar is important in the definition of the need for reform in the region, its major findings are reported in some detail.

Summary of the Major Results of the Sydney Symposium on Corporate Governance

While the corporation as an entity and corporate governance practices in general have been matters of domestic policy interest for many decades, the broader concept of corporate governance and its relationship to a wide range of private sector activities has moved to the forefront of international thinking only in the past few years.

The corporation today is responsible for generating the major part of world economic activity. It is a prominent player in all markets, ranging from goods and services to capital and human resources. The ability of a corporation to attract investments, generate profits, and create employment has direct bearing on the economic prosperity of the country wherein it is located.

The Asian economic crisis and the collapse of regional capital markets have focused attention on fundamental regulatory weaknesses in Asia's financial and corporate sectors. Concerns relating to unsound investment practices, poor standards of disclosure and accountability of large corporations, and the degree to which these contributed to the recent economic destabilization of the Asia-Pacific region, are now being aired. To revive investor confidence and help restore economic stability, government officials and business people are in the process of reforming corporate governance structures in Asian businesses.

1. *Sound corporate governance is the assurance that assets are managed in the best interests of owners and stakeholders.* Participants in the Corporate Governance in APEC Symposium agreed to the following basic principles of sound corporate governance:

- Timely and accurate disclosure of financial and, in some instances, non-financial performance records;
- Equitable treatment of all shareholders;
- Establishment of clear rights and responsibilities of shareholders, directors and managers; and

- Establishment of effective and enforceable accountability standards to help uphold sound management and decision-making processes.

The objective of the Corporate Governance in APEC Symposium was to emphasize cooperative efforts which could support financial system and corporate reform strategies. In this vein, symposium participants discussed the corporate governance challenges which face the region as a whole. While acknowledging unique and individual problems which face each economy, they focused on outlining governance difficulties which are common across the region. Immediate issues of concern among participants included:

- Allocating reduced flows of investment more efficiently;
- Creating more stable corporate financing structures that are less prone to future external shocks;
- Re-capitalizing viable companies and financial institutions;
- Regaining international private sector investor and lender confidence in the region;
- Deepening domestic equity markets; and
- Improving management and risk assessment practices among financial and corporate institutions.

Regional governments have important roles to play in developing good corporate governance policies and helping to implement appropriate reform measures. Symposium participants examined ways in which Asian governments could actively promote this process.

2. *Governments have a fundamental role to play in achieving corporate governance reforms, particularly in fostering leadership in business and professional communities with respect to this objective.* In recent years, as Asian companies expanded and increased their borrowings, not enough attention was given to the adjustment of governance practices. While corporate collapses have forced banks and lending institutions to consider corporate governance arrangements more fully before investments are made, there remains some resistance among businesses to alter their management practices.

Participants in the Corporate Governance in APEC Symposium discussed the need for all businesses to uphold certain standards of transparency and accountability. In recognition of the closed nature of many Asian business operations, participants recommended that governments take a lead role among business and professional groups in ensuring that companies meet appropriate reporting and disclosure standards.

3. *Governments should give high priority to the establishment of laws governing the sale of property, the design of contracts, and bankruptcy procedures. Governments should also legislate for good corporate accounting, auditing, and reporting standards.* Good corporate governance requires both a flexible market environment and clear and enforceable rules to guide sound business practices. Symposium participants underscored the need for policy-makers and regulators to play a lead role in enacting regulatory frameworks to ensure effective and efficient regulation of private sector operations.

Ownership structures of businesses, be they private, public, state, or family-owned, are key determinants of governance arrangements. In some instances, ownership is held by active and directly involved partners, while in other instances, owners are less involved.

Similar to predominant business structures which existed in the United States and Europe earlier in the last century, many Asian businesses today are owned, operated, and managed primarily by individual families. As a result, decisions relating to employment, management, investment, and accountability practices tend to be made in-house.

Participants in the Corporate Governance in APEC Symposium outlined the following legal issues which need to be addressed to effectively implement reform and safeguard against future financial turmoil:

- The establishment of internationally acceptable accountancy and auditing standards for companies;
- Development of reporting and disclosure regimes both at national and company levels;
- The establishment of laws regulating the duties of directors;
- The establishment of laws regulating related party transactions;
- Clear definition of shareholder and creditor rights and management responsibility;
- The creation of laws to govern property dealings, development of contracts, and bankruptcy procedures;
- The development of necessary infrastructure to effectively enforce new corporate laws;
- The creation of reliable and accessible court systems or other dispute settlement mechanisms; and
- The establishment of strong and reliable regulatory authorities.

4. *Governments should create public infrastructure necessary to assist in the effective application of corporate and commercial laws, including independent legal systems, prominent, well-resourced regulatory agencies, and professionally trained court officers.* As governments in Asia begin the task of addressing problems in the area of corporate governance, legal and regulatory frameworks are demanding

immediate attention. Regulatory bodies are being established in the most affected countries to protect shareholder and creditor rights and to promote management accountability. However, symposium participants stressed that the effective operation of regulatory and judicial authorities entrusted with administering and enforcing laws will depend on each authority being properly resourced, staffed by high quality personnel and operated in a fair and open manner. Governments must take responsibility for supporting this process.

5. *Governments should improve the competitiveness of goods and capital markets.* An open and dynamic private sector is fundamental to the economic stability of both industrialized and developing economies. Competitiveness is a key factor in maintaining the sector's energy and growth.

Several symposium participants noted that for the best performing companies to attract financing, the overall framework of goods and capital markets must be competitive. An open, transparent, and competitive market environment will help ensure that well-managed companies receive funding with lower risk premia than poorly managed and higher risk companies.

6. *Symposium participants urged APEC Leaders and Finance Ministers to support the development of the APEC collaborative initiative to improve corporate governance practices throughout the Asia-Pacific region.* Participants indicated that the broad APEC initiative, led by Malaysia and aimed at improving corporate governance in the Asia-Pacific region, should build on the outcomes of the Sydney Symposium. With additional research being undertaken by the World Bank and the Asian Development Bank, participants recommended that APEC Finance Ministers:

- Commit to high priority domestic reform measures in the area of corporate governance;
- Examine the types of international assistance available to further their efforts; and
- Utilize the political support offered through APEC to assist in achieving reforms.

Specific proposals for improvements in the area of corporate governance were outlined by symposium participants. (Drawn from Australian APEC Study Centre, 1998.)

ABAC Capacity-Building Task Force

In its 1999 report to the APEC Leaders, ABAC proposed the overhaul of APEC's economic and technical cooperation activities by installing a new programme which is more coherent than the current bundle of projects. The focus should be on capacity-building in support of the transition to more open markets.

ABAC argued that capacity-building in corporate governance was a key priority. It supported the initiative to set up the Core Group on Corporate Governance, and strongly endorsed programmes of work designed to improve capacity in this area. It suggested a collective activity in the form of peer assessment of corporate governance arrangements. Reaching new standards will reduce the vulnerability of business in the region and lower its cost of funds. It proposed a survey of capacity-building needs, as identified by member economies, in the area of economic governance.

Asian Bankers' Association

In 1999 the Asian Bankers' Association made a report to APEC Leaders on corporate debt restructuring after the crisis. A set of principles for debt restructuring was set out, and this included some recommendations on corporate governance. It drew attention to the need for urgent action in areas such as bankruptcy procedures, corporate governance, transparency and disclosure, director liability laws, and accountancy procedures.

The Pacific Economic Cooperation Council (PECC)

In April 2000, the PECC released a special paper prepared by Dr. Jesus P. Estanislao on "Strengthening Financial Markets and Corporate Governance". He argued that corporate governance is really about:

— the separation of powers between directors, managers, and shareholders. An effective system of checks and balances is necessary for fairness, accountability, and transparency.
— making the board of directors more effective.
— bringing an open, participatory system into the corporate boardroom.
— the development of effective risk management systems within a competitive market framework.

Report to APEC Finance Ministers, May 1999

As was noted above, in May 1999, a report on corporate governance was sent to APEC Finance Ministers, a result of the work of the APEC Collaborative Initiative in Corporate Governance. It drew heavily for its conceptual framework on the 1998 Sydney symposium. The starting point was the observation that many of the firms most seriously caught up in the crisis were characterized by high levels of indebtedness, imprudent financial and business practices, non-transparent ownership, and a lack of accountability to investors. Thus, there is real need to catch up with rapidly improving international standards. The report argued that an effective system of corporate governance is one that meets two basic criteria: *accountability* to shareholders, creditors, employees and customers; and *efficiency*, operating in the best interests of shareholders and in compliance with legal and regulatory requirements. The governance system should facilitate a number of key processes:

- participation by shareholders;
- oversight and monitoring of management;
- transparency and disclosure of relevant and timely information on company performance; and
- incentives for motivating management in the best interests of the owners.

Impediments to corporate governance have usually involved failures in safeguards for the rights of shareholders; the performance of boards of directors; transparency and accountability; and awareness of shareholders as to their rights. Thus, the most important factors conditioning corporate governance appear to be:

- ownership dispersal or concentration;
- board attributes;
- supporting checks and balances;
- the adequacy of legal and regulatory frameworks;
- accounting and auditing standards;
- product market competitiveness;
- efficiency of financial markets;
- competitiveness of managerial job markets; and
- a range of cultural and historical factors.

The report considered the adequacy of corporate governance systems in Asia, noted the wide variations between countries, and identified some serious problems in a number of countries. A key recommendation was the drawing up of voluntary action plans to give effect to commitments in member economies to domestic corporate governance reform. The aims of these plans should be the achievement of some key objectives:

- restoring the confidence of foreign investors in the region;
- promoting transparency in corporate procedures and accountability;
- increasing efficiency in investment and promoting domestic equity market development;

- creating more stable corporate and financing structures;
- recapitalizing viable companies and financial institutions; and
- improving management and risk assessment practices.

Finally, the report investigated the measures that should be taken by governments as well as companies to realize these objectives.

Actions Taken at the Level of Member Economies

It is not possible at this time to give a proper report on measures taken at the national level. As was noted earlier, the process of APEC involvement in this area is still in its early stages. Efforts have been directed to the definition of the problem and the design of a range of possible reforms. The policy roundtables planned for 2001 will take this a stage further and hopefully set the scene for national responses and possible individual action plans.

Evaluation

Again, it is difficult to present a reasonable evaluation given the early stage of the process of APEC involvement in this issue. Only one completed questionnaire was received, from Chile. The view was that given its loose organization, APEC had done as much as it could in the area of corporate governance. Training and human resource development are key areas where APEC can make a contribution. The sharing of information, skills and experience are important, and some "centres of excellence" should be established as a model.

Recommendations

The conceptual and definitional work on corporate governance begun by APEC is extremely useful and important, and should be continued. It is also vital, at the appropriate time, to move to the next stage which will involve national level reforms, perhaps through the vehicle of individual action plans. However, care must be taken not to exacerbate divisions between Asian and Western members of APEC. There already exists in the region a reaction against the highly unpopular interventions after the crisis by the International Monetary Fund. The United States, in particular, has been closely identified with these policies, and this has given rise to what some commentators have called the "politics of resentment" (Higgott 2000). These reactions have probably been intensified by what has been perceived as a Western superiority in these matters, often bordering on triumphalism. It is clear that a reaction is setting in, one which threatens cooperation in the wider region. A number of Asian commentators have pointed out that not all Asian companies were equally affected by the crisis, and have also argued that several countries in Asia have quickly returned to healthy growth rates even in the absence of any fundamental corporate reform. Hence, they argue, other factors must have been central to the crisis, notably the imperfect architecture of the international financial system. Success in this area will therefore require a great deal more sensitivity and theoretical sophistication than has been demonstrated to date.

References

Alba, P., A. Bhattacharya, S. Claessens, S. Ghosh, and L. Hernandez. "The Role of Macroeconomic and Financial Sector Linkages in East Asia's Financial Crisis". In *The Asian Financial Crisis: Causes, Contagion and Consequences,* edited by P-R. Agenor, M. Miller, D. Vines and A. Weber, pp. 9–64. Cambridge: Cambridge University Press, 1999.

Ang Swee Hoon, Lee Soon Hoon, Lim Guan Hua, Kulwant Singh and Tan Kong Yam. *Surviving the New Millennium: Lessons from the Asian Crisis.* Singapore: McGraw-Hill, 2000.

Australian APEC Study Centre. *Corporate Governance in APEC: Rebuilding Asian Growth.* Melbourne: Australian APEC Study Centre, with AusAID and the Australian Treasury, 1998.

Backman, Michael. *Asian Eclipse: Exposing the Dark Side of Business in Asia.* Singapore: John Wiley, 1999.

Haggard, Stephen. *The Political Economy of the Asian Financial Crisis.* Washington: Institute for International Economics, 2000.

Higgott, R. "The International Relations of the Asian Economic Crisis: A Study in the Politics of Resentment". In *Politics and Markets in the Wake of the Asian Crisis,* edited by R. Robison, M. Beeson, K. Jayasuria and H. R. Kim. pp. 261–82. London: Routledge, 2000.

Kotler, P. and J. Kartajaya. *Repositioning Asia: From Bubble to Sustainable Economy.* Singapore: John Wiley, 2000.

On Kit Tam. *The Development of Corporate Governance in China.* Cheltenham: Edward Elgar, 1999.

Vines, Stephen. *The Years of Living Dangerously: Asia from Financial Crisis to the New Millennium.* London: Orion Business Books, 1999.

12

FINANCIAL STABILITY IN THE APEC REGION

MICHAEL G. PLUMMER

Importance of Financial Stability Issues to APEC

The Asian crisis of 1997–99 was, by almost all measures, devastating. While a number of scholars claim to have anticipated an Asian crisis of some sort, no one seems to have expected its magnitude and severity, and, arguably, its exact substance. APEC was certainly taken by surprise. The organization's focus and greatest accomplishments had been mostly in the areas of trade, direct foreign investment, and in other regional policies designed to lower transaction costs. Until the Asian crisis, little attention had been directed strictly to financial matters.

In fact, APEC never had pretensions to be a regional grouping with a financial core; priorities were concentrated in the areas of trade and investment liberalization and facilitation and, to a lesser extent, development cooperation (eventually referred to as Ecotech). Other successful regional cooperation initiatives generally ignored financial areas. Nevertheless, the Asian crisis forced APEC to concentrate more on finance. APEC Summits during this period were dominated by consultation regarding the crisis and what to do about it. APEC financial officials suddenly became far more active and, certainly, their mission became more pressing.

During the Asian crisis and continuing to date, financial officials have discussed the need to work on a number of areas to strengthen financial stability in the region. These commitments are generally articulated in financial committee reports and communiqués. Clearly, APEC officials agree that the region should be actively involved in supporting regional financial stability. But how pressing is the need at present? How much progress has been made? What has APEC as an organization done and what might it do?

In order to answer some of these questions, an assessment questionnaire was developed as part of the APIAN project to capture ideas that experts in the region might have with respect to financial stability and the role of APEC. Below, we summarize the results from this questionnaire.

Questionnaire Analysis

The APIAN financial stability questionnaire was designed essentially to identify salient problems under the (perhaps overly-general) rubric of "financial stability", take stock of progress in strengthening financial stability in wake of the Asian crisis, and, in particular, focus on APEC's role in the past, present, and future in this area. The questionnaire was based on concerns gleaned from the literature and issues raised by APEC financial officials, in particular drawing on insights, goals, and expectations developed during the Auckland meetings in 1999.[1]

In preparing the questionnaire, we found that the Finance Ministers have not been reticent in trying to focus on problems and seek effective solutions, including at national, regional, and global levels. Much of the information that one finds is as applicable to regional as global cooperation. Coupled with the common principle of "open regionalism", this tendency to consider APEC approaches in a global context is what one would expect from such discussions. And, arguably, financial issues tend to be more "global" than issues related to the real sector.

However, it is also important to note that there is not a great deal of information regarding consultation and progress on issues related to financial-stability discussions in APEC. Many of the respondents to the questionnaires did not have much to say with respect to measures and polices already taken by APEC in various areas. It is likely that this is because knowledge of such activities is scarce. And if the associated experts were not particularly well informed, no doubt awareness among the interested general public would be even less. Certainly, dissemination of more information in easily-accessible format would enhance education in this area and, hopefully, serve as a basis for greater discussion, interaction, and research.

An essential problem with APEC cooperation in the area of finance, as was noted in a few of the questionnaires, is that APEC was not really created for this purpose: the bias has been towards facilitating and liberalizing trade and direct foreign investments, as well as ancillary "nuts-and-bolts" issues useful to improve business interaction and lower transaction costs in the region. In this sense, it has been argued in the literature, policy-related discussions, and academic meetings (for example, of the APEC Study Centre Consortium conferences) that it is inappropriate to criticize APEC's general lack of preparation and readiness in responding to the Asian crisis. After all, far more ambitious regional organizations in terms of economic integration (such as the European Community [EC] and the North America Free Trade Agreement [NAFTA]) have either ignored financial-stability issues, or had to spend a great deal of time in integrating the real sector before turning to finance.

Nevertheless, one can argue that the APEC experience is unique in that it includes major developed countries and major developing countries, highly-sophisticated financial systems and under-developed ones, and substantial capital exporters and importers. Such diversity might change the "natural" balance of the regional organization in favour of closer cooperation in financial areas. Given the close relationship between trade and finance and the rising degree of interdependence as a result of policy liberalization, inclusion of financial issues seems not only logical but, perhaps, necessary. For example, when the Mexican financial crisis began in December 1994, this became a critical issue in NAFTA, which had been almost entirely focused on integration in trade, direct foreign investment, and related issues.

In any event, it is obvious that public opinion expected much from APEC during the Asian crisis and was disappointed by its actions, regardless of the fact that finance was not explicitly APEC's domain. No doubt, APEC leaders did focus on containing the Asian crisis but there is wide-spread perception that the organization could have done more, a reaction also articulated by most of the respondents to the questionnaire.

Results of the Questionnaire by Topic

Only five questionnaires were completed and submitted to APIAN. Hence, the sample is small and cannot be construed as representative of all APEC countries. Of course, even if every APEC country had filled out a questionnaire, the results would still have required cautious interpretation, as obviously there exist differences of opinion within countries as well as between them.

A particular problem with this sample, however, is that there is insufficient representation of low- and middle-income countries. This is likely due to the short time that the country experts had to fill out the questionnaire. As low- and middle-income countries were generally the hardest hit by the Asian crisis, we would expect the results of the survey to be biased towards a more optimistic reading of the financial-stability *status quo* than otherwise would have been the case in some areas.

Despite the small sample, the experts from the five countries who did fill out the questionnaire gave excellent insights into the status of financial stability in their respective countries, as well as their assessment of the progress APEC has made in the area of financial stability. They also made a number of useful suggestions for the future.

In what follows, we give a summary of results by theme. In the final section, we draw some conclusions.

General Questions

Three of the countries that filled out the questionnaires were high-income countries, and two were middle-income. Four of the countries deemed that their respective countries were moderately affected by the Asian crisis, and only one (a middle-income country) believed that it had been severely affected. All experts said that their country's financial system prior to the crisis and currently was strong, with one exception in which the respondent considered it moderately sound before and after. All were optimistic about the future except one (high-income) country, which was somewhat pessimistic.

With respect to the role that APEC should play in fostering greater regional stability, there was, perhaps, a surprising diversity of opinion, with one expert (high-income country) advocating a highly-active role, three an active role, and one (middle-income) a restrictive role. A few suggested that APEC's role might be enhanced through more discussion of key issues (for example, on possible guidelines, such as contingency measures and legal and/or financial aid, which can be made available in times of regional financial instability) and information sharing. The expert who advocated a more restrictive role for APEC said that "too many cooks spoil the broth" but did see a role for sponsoring and encouraging training in APEC.

There was also considerable diversity regarding assessments of APEC's accomplishments so far in creating greater stability: Two (middle- and high-income) considered them important; one (middle-income) somewhat important; and two (middle- and high-income) unimportant. Criticisms included an assessment that APEC had currently only succeeded in focusing on public relations, information sharing, and needs, but with no agreements in these areas at such meetings. One noted that lack of agreement between major developed member-states impeded progress.

Prudential Regulation of Financial Institutions

Most experts expressed that their respective countries had made either excellent or very good progress in improving prudential regulations and strengthening risk management, with only one noting that initiatives had been merely adequate. Most countries did not think that highly-leveraged financial institutions threatened stability, but one expert did believe that his/her country had problems in the "pre-need" industry.

Four of the five respondents believed that APEC's role in promoting stronger prudential regulation in the region had been *disappointing*, and only one considered it to be adequate. Clearly, the respondents see a greater role for APEC in this area. However, a few experts did note that APEC had helped with respect to consultation and training, and one expressed concern that APEC had not done enough to increase public awareness of regional interdependence, which restricted its ability to solve regional problems. Regarding which initiatives to pursue, the respondents listed a number of options, including: creating "focus groups" within APEC with resources to back them; following arrangements spelled out in the Manila Framework; becoming active in truly regional issues and concentrating on prudential regulation together with APEC's liberalization agenda; harmonizing differences in disclosure requirements for local and international institutions, as well as favouring greater transparency; establishing more effective monitoring and enforcement units to check on the progress of member states; and in the wake of the Asian crisis, placing more emphasis on proper laws and regulations related to bankruptcy, debt restructuring, and mergers and acquisitions.

Transparency Issues

Respondents noted that transparency and disclosure standards in their respective financial institutions were good to very good. Areas where problems remain in some countries include banks (two countries), stockbrokers, "pre-need" plans, and small and medium-sized financial institutions that are dominated by a few major shareholders. Since the Asian crisis, the experts maintained that transparency had either remained the same (two countries) or become more transparent. APEC's contributions in this regard included creating increased awareness of interdependence, closer scrutiny of non-performing loans (NPLs), and better data on debt exposure. One respondent insisted that, besides asserting support, APEC had not done much.

Regarding suggestions as to what APEC might do, respondents gave a number of interesting ideas. Two experts underlined the need to encourage/organize activities devoted to "best practices" in corporate governance and in handling crises; others noted the need for common guidelines in a region that is so diverse, as well as more focus on research, perhaps including the creation of a regional research centre. One expert identified a need to promote additional Ecotech areas, including training of supervisers and off-site examiners (especially for developing-country central banks). One expert also suggested that APEC should address corruption-related issues.

Short-term Capital Flows

Most experts considered their country to be either highly-open or open to short-term capital flows, with one gauging that his/her country was somewhat closed. Four out of five said that the *status quo* regarding short-term capital-flow liberalization was just right, but one expert (high-income) judged his/her country to be too open. No expert believed that APEC had played an important role in promoting "safe, sustainable capital flows" in the region, with respondents noting that it was either very limited or had no significance at all. With respect to what role should be played, there was considerable disagreement among the experts, reflecting in general the difference of opinion between economists and financial experts in this area, with one respondent advocating taxation of short-term capital movements ("Tobin's plan"), one advocating greater liberalization, and another noting the need to focus on monitoring (rather than restrictions alone).

International Financial Architecture and Miscellaneous

Access to international capital flows for individual countries were deemed by the experts to vary from very good to excellent, with one (high-income) country suggesting it was merely sufficient. Global institutions focusing on financial-crisis management were essentially derided by all: most said they were insufficient and one said that they were destructive, noting that "one size fits all" policies do not work. Three experts believed that the current "hybrid" exchange-rate regime was "moderately beneficial", but comments generally suggested that this was because of the lack of a viable alternative, even in theory. One expert said that the system was detrimental. Two experts felt that the International Monetary Fund's (IMF's) Supplemental Reserve Facility and Contingent Credit Line were not sufficient to promote financial stability; rather, a regional approach was needed to supplement the IMF's resources (but one expert noted that it is important to keep in mind problems associated with the "moral hazard" problem, that is, too much support may decrease incentives to implement sufficient domestic preventative measures). One expert said that the IMF was the source of the problem, stressing the need to make regulatory capital bases higher, and imposing greater penalties on excessive risk-taking banks.

With respect to the future role that respondents felt APEC might play in enhancing financial-crisis management, once again there was a diversity of opinion. One expert insisted on the need to replicate OECD capacity. Another noted the need to pool resources, and yet another focused on the need to promote currency stability and coordination, especially with respect to "informal" currency blocs in areas characterized by subregional preferential agreements (for example, ASEAN, NAFTA).

Conclusions

The Asian crisis was a tragedy, especially in its effect on the poorest of the poor in the Asia-Pacific region. However, as the region is now (for the most part) recovering from the crisis and is growing at a respectable — if not yet pre-crisis — rate, it is imperative that we do not ignore what happened during the crisis and, in finding the answers, to work towards promoting policies to prevent or at least manage more effectively any future crisis. As the Asian crisis was largely financial in nature, working to strengthen financial stability is of the essence.

The critical need to improve financial stability in the region seems to be underscored by all: APEC leaders, other policy-makers, private-sector representatives, and academia. APEC has placed a stronger emphasis on financial matters in general, and financial stability in particular. It is hoped that this attention will continue, as isolating "real" from "financial" matters holds many perils.

The experts responding to the financial stability questionnaire offered an interesting set of insights into the state of the region, what APEC has done, and what it can do in the future. There is no consensus on policy prescriptions; however, it would appear that most believe in a much stronger role for APEC in this area, especially since most believe that APEC has hitherto done very little in terms of concrete results (but, of course, this is due in part to the fact that APEC was not originally conceived as a "financial" organization). As all seem to think that global institutions have been either ineffective or downright destructive, the role for APEC as a regional institution in confronting the myriad problems associated with financial stability appears to be justified as a complement to (perhaps reformed) global institutions. This opinion also seems to be reflected in the meetings of the APEC Study Centres and associated research; while there appears to be no consensus on the exact types of policies that need to be pursued, there is agreement that more can be done. Moreover, the need to improve consultation, information-sharing, training, and various Ecotech-related activities, with resources to support them, is shared by most. Perhaps this is the best place to start.

APPENDIX

QUESTIONNAIRE ON FINANCIAL STABILITY IN APEC

Definition of Initiative, Purpose and Targets

While financial stability was not originally a key area of cooperation in APEC, the Asian financial crisis of 1997–99 convinced the APEC leaders of the need to place issues related to the smooth and effective functioning of financial markets and institutions at the top of the agenda. Currently, there exists no formal commitments/targets within APEC regarding the strengthening of financial markets and institutions at the national and regional levels (as in the case, for example, of trade and investment). However, the Finance Ministers have issued a number of reports and declarations in which they express their solidarity regarding the need to enhance cooperation and to ameliorate the existing financial system through concerted initiatives. Priority areas include: prudential regulation of financial institutions, transparency and disclosure standards for private sector financial institutions, complications related to short-term capital flows, enhancing supervision and deepening financial markets, and improving crisis management.

Evaluation of Effective Progress in Home Country and APEC-Wide

The purpose of this questionnaire is to: (1) evaluate the effectiveness (and appropriateness) of new financial-stability initiatives taken since the crisis, as part of national and APEC-wide initiatives; and (2) assist the APEC Leaders in identifying additional areas in which further cooperation would be beneficial to regional stability, as well as highlight shortcomings in the existing agenda.

Assessment of Strengths and Weaknesses

I. General Questions

1. Your country would be classified as:
   Low Income   Middle Income   High Income

2. The Asian crisis affected your country:
   Severely   Moderately   Mildly   Not-at-All

3. You would characterize the stability of your country's financial system PRIOR to the Asian crisis to have been:
   Strong   Moderate   Weak

4. You would characterize the stability of your country's financial system TODAY to be:
   Strong Moderate Weak

5. With respect to the future of your country's financial system, you are:
   Highly-Optimistic Optimistic Somewhat-Pessimistic Pessimistic

6. In general, the role of APEC in fostering greater regional financial stability should be:
   Highly-Active Active-Restricted Highly-Restricted

   COMMENT

7. You would gauge APEC's contribution to date in fostering greater regional financial stability to be:
   Highly-Important Important Somewhat-Important Unimportant

   COMMENT

II. Prudential Regulation of Financial Institutions

8. In your view, your country's initiatives at the national level to improve prudential regulation of financial institutions have been:
   Excellent Very-Good Adequate Inadequate

9. You would characterize your country's risk-management practices to be:
   Excellent Very-Good Adequate Inadequate

10. Do highly-leveraged financial institutions in your country threaten stability? If so, please explain briefly where the most important problems exist.

11. APEC's role in promoting stronger prudential regulation in the region has been:
    Impressive Adequate Disappointing

(For questions 12-13). APEC's role in helping to strengthen prudential regulation could vary extensively, from merely sharing information to adopting regional standards.

12. In your view, which have been the most important APEC initiatives in this area?

13. In your view, how involved do you believe that APEC should be in pursuing such initiatives? Please also give a few examples of initiatives that APEC might pursue in the future.

OTHER COMMENTS ON PRUDENTIAL SUPERVISION

III. Transparency Issues

14. You would rate the transparency and disclosure standards for your country's financial institutions to be:
    Excellent Very-Good Good Acceptable Problematic Highly-Problematic

15. In your country, in which types of financial institutions are transparency problems the most salient?

16. With respect to transparency since the Asian crisis began, your country has become:
    Much-More-Transparent More-Transparent Stayed-the-Same Less Transparent

17. What have been APEC's most important contributions (if any) in helping promote greater transparency of financial institutions?

18. What sort of activities do you believe that APEC could pursue in the future in this area?

OTHER COMMENTS ON TRANSPARENCY ISSUES

IV. Short-Term Capital Flows

20. With respect to the openness of short-term capital flows prior to the Asian crisis, you would have classified your country as being:
    Highly-Open Open Somewhat-Closed Closed

21. Today, you would classify your country's openness to short-term capital flows to be:
    Highly-Open Open Somewhat-Closed Closed

22. With respect to the liberalization of short-term capital flows, you feel that your country is:
    Too-Open Just-Right Too-Closed

    COMMENTS

23. What role do you feel that APEC has played in promoting "safe, sustainable capital flows" in the region?

24. What sort of constructive initiatives might APEC play in this regard in the future?

    OTHER COMMENTS ON SHORT-TERM CAPITAL FLOWS

V. International Financial Architecture and Miscellaneous

25. You would rate the access of your country to international capital flows to be:
    Excellent Very-Good Sufficient Insufficient

26. With respect to financial-crisis management, you would rate existing global institutions to be:
    Excellent Very-Good Sufficient Insufficient Destructive

    COMMENTS

27. From your country's perspective, you would rate the current "hybrid" system of exchange-rate regimes to be:
    Beneficial Moderately-Beneficial Somewhat-Detrimental Detrimental

28. It has been argued that the IMF's Supplemental Reserve Facility and Contingent Credit Line should play an important part in promoting financial stability. Are these sufficient? If not, would you favour a regional approach as well?

29. Do you feel that APEC's response to the Asian crisis was appropriate? Please explain briefly.

30. What future role do you feel that APEC might play in enhancing financial crisis management (if any)?

OTHER COMMENTS

Recommendations

These questionnaires are being distributed to all APEC Study Centres and will be used as input to an APIAN Report on Financial Stability. In addition to providing an *ex-post* review of national and APEC-wide progress in this area, the Report will also include a series of recommendations to APEC Leaders. It would be very useful if you could provide some suggestions as to additional areas in which APEC might become active in fostering greater financial stability, and/or how it might improve on existing initiatives.

Notes

1. For example, see *Report of APEC Finance and Central Bank Deputies on Strengthening International Financial Architecture* (Auckland, New Zealand, 8 September 1999), available through the APEC Secretariat webpage.
2. With this financial eruption on its borders, and in part due to the newly-established NAFTA, the United States rushed to Mexico's aid, marshalling together approximately US$40 billion to stem the crisis.
3. A copy of the questionnaire is available from the author upon request.

13

APEC AS AN INSTITUTION[1]

VINOD K. AGGARWAL AND KUN-CHIN LIN

Summary of Key Initiatives

During the past decade, APEC's momentum has waxed and waned with its impact on policy-making and trade liberalization. An important high-point was the 1993 meeting in Seattle, attended by leaders of the APEC economies, elevating APEC from a sleepy forum for Foreign and Trade Ministers to a much more visible summit-level activity. Some viewed this development as a sign of APEC's coming of age as well as an effective means of putting pressure on the Europeans to come to an agreement in the Uruguay Round. The 1994 meeting in Bogor, Indonesia, led to a call for free trade and investment in the area by 2010 for the developed APEC member economies, and 2020 for the entire group. A framework of guiding principles was agreed to the following year in Osaka and in 1996 APEC adopted an Action Plan involving unilateral concerted liberalization as well as collective actions. The group also agreed to press for a World Trade Organization (WTO) breakthrough on information technology. Its political success in pushing forward the Information Technology Agreement (for which much of the work had already been done in other contexts) encouraged APEC to move ahead with other "early voluntary sectoral liberalization" (EVSL) schema. The 1997

Vancouver meeting agreed to implement EVSL in nine sectors, thus holding out hope for a major role for APEC as a key adjunct to the WTO for promoting trade liberalization.

By 1998, however, APEC's role and the use of the sectoral approach to liberalization had come into sharp scrutiny. By the time of the Kuala Lumpur meetings (some would say even by the time of Vancouver) it was clear that APEC had failed to play a significant role in ameliorating the Asian financial crisis. The EVSL effort faltered as Japan and several other countries objected to the liberalization of some sectors in the context of the economic crisis, and in the face of U.S. pressure for sectoral concessions and reciprocity. The tension and uncertainties arising from a lack of consensus in the APEC forum carried over to the Seattle WTO Summit in November 1999 and the aftermath of its political showdown, further polarizing the public positions of APEC members along the fault-line of environmental and labour linkages to trade issues.

Throughout 2000, APEC members expressed commitment to multilateralism while in practice turned to bilateralism in trade negotiations. Singapore has been the most active, engaging in bilateral talks with Japan, New Zealand, Canada, Chile, and Mexico towards creating free trade agreements (FTA). Each of these countries negotiating an FTA with Singapore is at the same time pursuing other bilateral deals within the Asia-Pacific region. Most importantly, Japan, although its government ministries are still somewhat divided on this issue, has also begun to get in the act; only the United States is notably absent from this bilateral agenda (at least until a flurry of activity — with Singapore and Chile — in the closing days of the Clinton Administration). It remains to be seen whether these bilateral deals will turn out to be building blocks or stumbling blocks towards trans-Pacific free trade.[2]

These negative developments and concerns about APEC's ability to foster liberalization have been accompanied by more sceptical criticism from those analysts who view APEC as positively harmful. They note that the Asia-Pacific region has become the most dynamic region in the world economy without any significant formal institutions, and argue that by encouraging further regionalization of the world economy, APEC might undermine the global economic regime, and hence deepen regional rivalry.

Actions Taken at the International Level

The most significant contributions of APEC have been in agenda-setting and socialization of member economies into the acceptance of global norms and principles. The scope of issues covered by APEC has expanded from the traditional areas of trade and investment liberalization to cutting-edge agenda, such as infrastructure, environmental protection, women's issues, and social problems. In the aftermath of the Asian crisis, the issue of regional financial coordination has also been added to the agenda.

The most significant area has been the creation, by the 1996 Osaka Action Plan, of Economic and Technical Co-operation (Ecotech), one of the main pillars of APEC's structure. The group was created to foster developments in technology and infrastructure in the hope of equalizing disparities and promoting sustainable economic growth for all member economies. On paper, Ecotech's scope covers developing human capital to safeguarding the quality of life through environmentally sound growth (Bergsten 1997, p. 141). In an attempt to remedy the problems of bilateral cooperation, a new model was implemented in which all interested members would participate in economic cooperation through the gathering of relevant information and policy promotion. Furthermore, official development of infrastructure was expanded to include private assistance in an effort to relieve the financial burden from the more developed member economies. The outcome of these reforms to Ecotech has led to a more responsive and effective model for economic development in which goals are better defined, implementation is regularly discussed, and performance measures are more easily monitored.

In the area of environmental protection, the framework that emerged from the seven years of APEC activities consists of the following components:

1. Agenda-setting by the Regional Environmental Cooperation Forum, producing a series of action programmes and strategies;
2. Working Groups and Committees mainly comprised of engineers who operationalize objectives and develop plans for public–private cooperation; and
3. "Capacity-building" seminars and workshops to enhance awareness, disseminate norms, and develop analytical abilities.

As mentioned above, the majority of APEC members prefer to avoid direct environmental and labour linkages to trade liberalization negotiation.

APEC has also incorporated women's issues into its committees and meetings. In the recent 1998 Senior Officials Meeting (SOM), there was a call for a "Framework for the Integration of Women in APEC", which would include guidelines for gender analysis, improvements to the collection and utilization of sex-disaggregated data and approaches to the involvement of women.[3]

APEC has also indicated a willingness to take on a greater role in addressing social problems arising from cross-border labour mobility and the Asian crisis. APEC's focus in this area has been confined to medium- and long-term preparation of the labour force for the global changes in labour demand; the regime's scope remains focused on the quality of basic education, analysis of the regional labour market, increasing the supply and quality of managers and entrepreneurs, and training geared towards liberalization and facilitation of trade and investments in the region. In the end, since workers' issues in APEC are currently nested in the trade and investment liberalization regime, concerns for economic efficiency are likely to trump any attempt to provide greater labour protection.

Another emerging issue discussed in the APEC forum is financial coordination. SOM meetings from Manila 1996 to Auckland 1999 have been dominated by financial issues arising from the Asian crisis. Many of the institutions in the Asia-Pacific have attempted to play an active role in salvaging crisis-ridden economies, but the International Monetary Fund (IMF), backed by the United States, has continued to assert its dominance. In the November 1997 Vancouver summit meeting, Leaders endorsed the so-called Manila framework, which called on the IMF to take the lead in providing emergency loans to Thailand, Indonesia, and South Korea, with APEC members playing only a secondary role to supplement IMF resources on a standby basis without any formal commitment of funds. Thus, with the APEC action providing the seal of the U.S.-IMF-backed plan, alternative institutional solutions were put on hold. In particular, Japan's and Malaysia's advocacy for an Asian Monetary Fund (AMF) was vehemently opposed by the United States as potentially undercutting the effectiveness of IMF conditionality.

Even before the economic crisis, APEC had been criticized for putting "too many eggs in the trade basket" (Morrison 1997, pp. 37–56). The fact is that APEC mushroomed into many other arenas, with ministerial meetings on finance, environment, transportation, energy, ocean policy, and other areas. However, because the Bogor vision privileged trade and the structure of APEC failed to provide representation for other than Trade and Foreign Ministers at the Leaders level, these other arenas have been generally sidelined. The most glaring example is finance. APEC Finance Ministers used to meet at almost the opposite side of the year from the Leaders' meetings. This indicates that their recommendations might not have been conveyed to the higher level in a timely manner. The result was that prior to the November 1997 Vancouver Ministerial and Leaders' meetings, APEC was in danger of having no plans relevant to the major financial crisis sweeping its Asian members.

Actions Taken at the National Level

The evidence that APEC has had a constraining and shaping influence on national policy action is insignificant. This is not surprising in the light of APEC's deliberate institutional design to eschew Western-style bureaucratization, and coercive implementation and enforcement measures. Such institutional limitations of APEC have reinforced the sceptics' belief that substantial rules-building at the broad Asia-Pacific level, separate from and in advance of the global level, is unlikely even as member economies respond to the same force of interdependence.

Nevertheless, the principles and norms of APEC may have had some influence on state policies. Studies indicate some cognitive similarity or convergence of expectation in the most engaged bureaucracies (basically Foreign and Trade Ministries) of the key APEC member economies. Those that once pursued strong import-substitution policies in the manufacturing sector, including China, most ASEAN countries, and Australia, have been unilaterally dismantling them. Moreover, the APEC economies, from different starting points and at different speeds, have all been moving towards further deregulation and privatization.

These liberalizing trends, of course, are not the direct result of the establishment of APEC but have their roots in the transformation of the global economy and national context as well. However, APEC's association with these trends has given them additional political strength within the national context. In fact, the national bureaucracies often look to APEC and each other for reinforcement of a liberal economic policy line against domestic interests who do not share the liberalizing ideology.[4]

Apart from the institutional limitations of APEC, national actions have been circumscribed by the domestic political institutions in some of the key APEC members. In initiating the EVSL, the United States had demanded explicit reciprocity even as other APEC members pointed to voluntarism as the APEC operating principle. This conflict is complicated by the U.S. Congress' withholding of fast-track authorization from President Clinton. The U.S. Congress requires reciprocity in its advance grant of authority to the President to engage in trade negotiations, and on non-tariff issues it has a second chance to ensure its standards of reciprocity after the negotiations through the need for its approval of the necessary implementing legislation.[5]

Japan's situation offers another example of domestic barriers to implementing APEC-level commitments. In Japan, the legislative process does not require a prior grant of authority, but political interest groups, including elements in the bureaucracy itself, have been quite effective in slowing or blocking liberalization in many sectors. The tried and true formula for moving ahead has usually been heavy-handed *gaiatsu*, or foreign pressure. While APEC might seem to make such pressures more acceptable by multilateralizing and "Asianizing" them, the limits of this became apparent in 1998 with the failure of APEC to complete an ESVL package because of resistance in the Japanese Ministry of Agriculture,

Forestry and Fisheries to a comprehensive package including forestry and fishery products.

As a result, APEC has been perceived among national commercial constituencies as a mere talking shop with little punch in driving real market opening within the Pacific Rim. Responding to this prevalent perception, Timothy Ong, chairman of the APEC Business Advisory Council (ABAC) argues that industries should moderate their expectations, given the diversity among the membership as well as the fact that APEC is the only realistic way that trade barriers can be lowered throughout the region.[6]

Assessment of Strengths and Weaknesses

In the light of the critical scrutiny and political uncertainties centred around APEC, we found it timely and useful to design a questionnaire to assess APEC as an institution. To this end, the questionnaire borrowed its conceptual framework from the existing work by Vinod Aggarwal (1998) and characterized APEC on its rules and procedures as well as its institutional structure. Respondents were asked to agree or disagree with our definitions and assessments of some important aspects of the APEC regime and institutions, and to provide open-ended elaboration on their viewpoints. Six completed questionnaires were received and their APEC member origin included the United States, Chile, Hong Kong, the Philippines, Singapore, and one anonymous membership. In what follows, we interpret their responses with reference to the major themes discussed above.

Interpretation of the Questionnaire Results

From the responses to the questionnaire, we find surprising concurrence on APEC's institutional weaknesses in the area of trade liberalization. Respondents disagree and show the greatest interest in areas such as Ecotech and APEC's issue and membership scopes, as well as the appropriate next-steps for the development of APEC.

Regime Characteristics

1. *Strength*
   a. Definition: The degree to which actor's behaviour is constrained by the rules and procedures and the specificity of the formal rules;
   b. Assessment: Persistence of deliberately weak institutionalization creates tension with APEC's highly liberal nature and broad issue scope.

Respondents generally agree with our definition and assessment. Several respondents focused on the negative, unintended consequences of the sectoral approach to trade liberalization, adopted at the 1997 Vancouver Summit upon the urging of the Clinton Administration. The EVSL created tension among APEC members, distracted the forum from the goals of the Bogor Accord, and went against the Osaka principle of comprehensiveness.

Respondents perceived the operational principle of decision-by-consensus as historically given, deriving it from the antecedent principle of ASEAN. While they are concerned with the slow progress of the consensual approach, they are willing to give it the benefit of the doubt that "the give and take in the approach may in fact be a long-term strength when outcomes are accepted with less tension and contention."

Criticisms of our interpretation are directed at our institutional process-oriented criteria that might have underestimated the inner coherence and external influence of APEC. One respondent criticizes our definition of "strength" for leaving no room for "assessing APEC's overall international authority, mandate and 'power'... [which] are important feedbacks for the actors who determine the rules, procedures and structures [of APEC]." The same respondent also showed reservation towards our assessment, arguing that "weak institutionalization" is a characterization that masks "a system of interlocking bureaucracies from different economies... [which have become] structurally embedded (strong) as an enduring unit and certainly will not blow down easily." At the same time, this respondent flatly stated that APEC "is no more liberal than the sum of its liberal and conservative [member] governments." Under this respondent's disaggregated view of the institution, the strength and weakness of APEC directly result from its horizontal organization and weak hierarchy. Even while bureaucrats take the opportunity to create their own domains based on loosely supervised projects and programmes, this horizontal growth and involvement of new actors serve as a "powerful, ever expanding regional integrative force." In sum, bureaucratic sprawl leads to institutional strength that might or might not fulfill desired institutional objectives.

2. *Nature*

   a. Definition: Objectives promoted by the regime (for example, liberalization)
   b. Assessment: The economic success of the Asia-Pacific economies has initially encouraged members to choose trade and investment liberalization to further increase competitiveness and efficiency in the region and to prevent other blocs from shutting out Asian exports. But it is unclear whether all members have a commitment to real liberalization or simply to border

reductions that would allow the continuation of export-oriented industrial policies. This ambiguity is underscored by the trade disputes in the aftermath of the Asian financial crisis and the collapse of the U.S.-led sectoral initiatives (EVSL).

Respondents place strong emphasis on the historical context of APEC formation. The goal of trade liberalization must be interpreted in that context, with the implication that it might vary when the initial conditions no longer hold. If APEC was initiated as a defensive reaction to regionalism elsewhere and to keep the United States committed to the growth of intra-Pacific trade, then the Asian crisis has modified this rationale since many economies have dropped the export-oriented industrial policies, and shifted efforts towards bilateral and subregional accords. One respondent predicts that, in the end, these changes are likely to lead to clearer definitions of APEC goals.

Some respondents are critical of our prioritization of the organizational goal of trade liberalization. One argues that Ecotech cooperation has emerged as an independent agenda, especially for developing member economies. Initially, Ecotech aimed solely to assist in the liberalization effort, but over time it has acquired a function independent of trade liberalization, one that covers human resource development and social impacts in the aftermath of the Asian crisis. Another respondent concurs that trade liberalization is actually "a weakening leg" of APEC. Other functions of information dissemination, education, trade facilitation and development cooperation are likely to prove more salient and productive in the long run. APEC is likely to grow into an OECD-like body, rather than an EU.

3. *Issue Scope*
   a. Definition: The number of issues included on the agenda
   b. Assessment: The number of issues has continued to increase despite the lack of institutionalization. Trade and investment liberalization remains the dominant objective of APEC, but social, financial coordination, environment and labour issues have been brought into the APEC agenda under a separate and secondary track. Security remains hotly contested, particularly in the light of the Indonesia-East Timor violence and the tumultuous cross-Taiwan Straits relations. It is unclear whether there is sufficient consensus among members on what should be placed on the agenda.

Respondents are generally in agreement with our definition and assessment, at least in principle. Nevertheless, one respondent challenged our ability to distinguish an "issue" from a "sub-issue" that might have resulted from a practical decision by some APEC committees to break up a complex issue. Thus, the proliferation of issues does not necessarily mean an expanding agenda, or over-extension of APEC institutional resources. In addition, this respondent argued that the number of issues was "a poor gauge of scope when various levels of decision-making are considered" — that is, the different prioritization and bundling of issues according to the leaders, ministers, committees, etc., defeat our organization-wide evaluation.

A division of labour, or horizontal linkages between international organizations, rather than incorporation of more issues under APEC, is the preferred future direction for all respondents. Labour and environmental issues should not be brought into the trade and investment agenda; instead, they should remain under the purview of the International Labour Organization (ILO). At most, APEC should focus on national capacity-building in achieving medium-term progress on these issues. Neither should security issues enter the APEC formal agenda; hence, respondents advise against nesting the ASEAN Regional Forum (ARF) under APEC. A respondent specified that "East Timor, Korean Peninsula, and cross-[Taiwan] Straits issues can be dealt at the ARF." In this regard, the involvement of Foreign Ministers is problematic.

However, a few respondents conceded that APEC could take on a limited role of preventing another financial crisis — by focusing mainly on developing research, an early warning system, and transparent fiscal practices, but avoiding plans for a regional monetary fund, monetary coordination, or exchange rate mechanisms. Others preferred to simply leave the financial issues to the IMF/World Bank, and have APEC deal narrowly with social impacts through its Human Resources Development Working Group (HRDWG).

4. *Membership Scope*

a. Definition: The number of APEC members, and civil society participation.

b. Assessment: First, there has been dispute over the widening of APEC. There is currently a moratorium on membership but several states in the region wish to join APEC. New members had been admitted before the institutionalization of accession conditionality. The history of European integration advises deepening before widening to keep the momentum of cooperation and convergence from flagging, but APEC has not followed such a sequencing scheme. Secondly, the scope of participation of APEC meetings has been largely confined to official representatives and bureaucrats, leaving NGOs, activists, and outside scientists to hold parallel conferences that do not contribute directly to APEC activities. In the light of U.S. President Bill Clinton's call for greater transparency and civil society participation in international trade organizations, in response to the mobilization at the Seattle WTO meeting, should APEC consider similar reforms?

Respondents are generally in agreement about the hazards in expanding membership scope, or "widening" of APEC. An optimistic respondent felt that "open regionalism" and the broad agenda of APEC could practically accommodate other economies such as India and Colombia before deepening cooperation. Another respondent was less tolerant:

> APEC's membership has been self-defeating. Several economies… are not capable of meeting the extensive demands that the organization places on its member bureaucracies for expertise and leadership. Moreover, group dynamics that worked well in the original smaller APEC membership have been seriously encumbered by the expansion.

Respondents registered strong disagreement over the desirability of and practical approach to civil society participation. One respondent preferred that APEC continue to build a constituency through business and academic networks. The extent of civil society participation should be left to the political process of each member economy. Democratic governments would naturally listen to their domestic groups; in closed societies, one can only hope that economic liberalization would contribute to internal openness over time. Another respondent pointed out that, more often than not, civil society views are dispersed, and thus there is no single authoritative voice to represent the civil society. Furthermore, where non-governmental organizations (NGOs) are involved in the APEC process, they have historically shown a lack of understanding of the process. One respondent pointed out that APEC has made efforts to increase transparency of its public discussions by having its reports made available on its website 30 days after the meeting — something that is not done by the WTO.

Another respondent objected to our premise that civil society participation has not been present in the APEC context. This respondent argued that civil society participation has had an early place in APEC history, but has been hampered by disputes among NGOs over the "legitimate voice of the people", as evidenced by the contentions among NGOs in 1996. Another respondent even argued that the "window dressing exercises" of conducting parallel women, youth, or even ABAC participation will eventually cripple and discredit the organization. However, no solution for genuine representation has been offered. This respondent was adamant that the Eminent Persons Group (EPG) was unlikely to provide an alternative to civic networks, as it was comprised of "a handful of willful [*sic.*] private individuals who will not respond so easily to control." Instead, the member governments have favoured ABAC "whose members are carefully selected by their governments and kept under relatively strict observation and control." In addition, to defray the costs of expensive annual events, APEC governments have offered a privileged role for multinational corporations in these events, to the exclusion of regional civic leaders and experts with contrary priorities. This trend will lead to a deterioration of the image of APEC.

Formal and Informal Institutional Structures

We asked the respondents to rank, in order of "high", "medium", or "low", the effectiveness of the following APEC institutions of negotiation, implementation, and administration. By "effectiveness", we refer to the institution's contribution to achieving the APEC goals of maintaining a forward liberal momentum based on consensus among member economies and consistency with the global trading regime of the WTO. In Table 1, we have provided a tally of responses and numerical averages based on the following ordinal rankings: "high" = 3 points, "medium" = 2 points, "low" = 1 point. The quantification is purely for the purpose of representing the mean of responses, and has no substantive value in itself. We caution our readers to keep in mind that the sample size (N=6) is insufficient to attempt any generalization.

Survey Responses on APEC as an Institution

Owing to the low number of responses, we cannot perform a quantitative analysis on the coded variables as we had originally designed. Nevertheless, we venture to identify some patterns and triangulate with responses from the questionnaires. The most persistent theme among the responses is a low opinion of the efficacy of the "negotiating modalities" of IAP, CAP, EVSL, and Early Harvest, of which EVSL received the worst rating from all but one respondent. Similarly, all but one respondent gave medium to low marks for institutions in overseeing implementation — we believe this indicates an underlying critical or ambivalent view towards the "voluntary" nature of APEC commitments. Among the "negotiating forum", working groups received low marks, which is surprising considering that these groups should provide the least politicized and most practical occasions for ironing out national differences. In comparison,

Table 1 **Survey Responses on APEC as an Institution**

Negotiating Forum	HIGH (3)	MEDIUM (2)	LOW (1)	AVERAGE
1. Leaders' Summits	IIIII	I		2.8
2. Ministerials	I	IIIII		2.2
3. Senior Official Meetings	I	IIIII		2.2
4. Committee on Trade and Investment		IIIII	I	1.8
5. Working Groups		II	IIII	1.3
Negotiating Modalities				
1. Individual Action Plans	I	IIII	I	2
2. Collective Action Plans	I	IIII	I	2
3. Early Voluntary Sectoral Liberalization		I	IIIII	1.2
4. Early Harvest		II	IIII	1.3
Oversight of Implementation				
1. Self-review		III	III	1.5
2. Peer-review	I	IIII	I	2
3. PECC/Trade Policy Forum studies		IIIII	I	1.8
Administrative Structures				
Secretariat	I	III	II	1.8

Leaders' summits are perceived as highly effective, since all major initiatives have been launched at the summits. Finally, respondents showed mixed feelings towards the Secretariat — those who considered working groups to be ineffective also gave higher than average credit to IAPs and CAPs, but tended to discount the usefulness of the Secretariat.

Recommendations

Our findings provide support for the following recommendations from Aggarwal and Morrison (2000):

1. Although APEC's vision of free trade and investment in the region by 2010/2020 may not be realized, this vision provides a stimulus for action that has been quite useful. The organization needs to grapple directly with how this vision can be realistically modified so that the trade ambitions do not exceed the institutional capacity

of the organization. It also needs to address how new governance mechanisms may help to strengthen APEC's ability to deliver on its objectives. These challenges require some extended and serious collective thinking — perhaps more than can be expected by the national bureaucratic mechanisms that are typically too caught up in day-to-day policy-making to engage in longer-term thinking.

2. APEC needs to have a clearer agenda of non-trade goals while limiting the scope of its activities to fewer priority areas. At a minimum, finance needs to be addressed more consistently and in a manner that more directly connects the Finance Ministries with the Leaders' Meetings.
3. The Leaders' Meetings are a significant feature of APEC, but reflect the more personalistic rather than institutionalized nature of the APEC process. For better or for worse, at this point these meetings are seen as the most effective negotiating forum for APEC. Thus, it is important that such meetings continue, both for the sake of the international relations of the region and to drive forward the APEC cooperation processes. Attention must be paid to ensuring that such meetings be perceived as valuable within national governments and taken seriously by heads of states.
4. Despite the APEC norms against EU-style bureaucratization, the APEC Secretariat needs to be strengthened by creating longer-term positions for the head of the Secretariat. Moreover, in-house research capabilities need to be enhanced to help APEC leaders set priorities as well as realistic targets.
5. Closer ties need to be developed between APEC and other regional and global organizations to facilitate wider and deeper cooperation. For the sake of APEC's long-run institutionalization, trends of sectoralism and bilateralism should not render the forum less relevant, and gains in liberalization from these alternative avenues of negotiations should be constructively nested under APEC.

Notes

1. For the first three sections, excerpts of analysis from Aggarwal and Morrison (2000) have been used.
2. *BASC News* 3, no. 2 (Summer/Fall 2000). As C. Fred Bergsten has recently argued in the *Economist* (15 July 2000), movements towards an East Asian Economic Caucus that were spurned only a few years ago are now being reconsidered by those in the region. To a certain extent, such a trend may be natural, considering the growing interdependence among East Asian economies. But disaffection with the United States — with its domineering

imposition of the Washington Consensus and growing fondness for including labour and environmental conditions on the trade agenda — is in no small part responsible for wanting to exclude the Americans from Asia's reviving economic boom. APEC, of which the United States is a member, is bound to suffer as a consequence of this ill-feeling. The trend towards bilateralism is both more benign and more limited than it may initially appear. On the other hand, the keen participation in bilateral talks of New Zealand, Chile, and Mexico suggests that such deals, if they do materialize, may indeed strengthen common interests among all APEC members, not just those within Asia. Meanwhile, for political reasons, it would be difficult to imagine a bilateral deal between Japan and China, by far the two most important economies in East Asia and the only pairing in the region that would have major trade-diversionary consequences for others in the Asia-Pacific.

3. *Business World*, 9 March 1999.
4. For a further discussion of China, see Zhang in Aggarwal and Morrison (1998), pp. 223–24.
5. For more details, see Aggarwal and Lin (forthcoming).
6. *BASC News* 3, no. 2 (Summer/Fall 2000).

References

Aggarwal, Vinod K. "Analyzing Institutional Transformation in the Asia-Pacific". In *Asia Pacific Crossroads: Regime Creation and the Future of APEC*, edited by Vinod K. Aggarwal and Charles E. New York: St. Martin's Press, 1998.

Aggarwal, Vinod K. and Kun-Chin Lin. "Strategy Without Vision: The U.S. and Asia-Pacific Economic Cooperation". In *The Asia Pacific Economic Cooperation: The First Decade*, edited by J. Ruland, E. Manske, and W. Draguhn. Forthcoming.

Aggarwal, Vinod K. and Charles E. Morrison. "APEC as an International Institution". In *Asia Pacific Economic Cooperation: Challenges and Tasks for the Twenty-first Century*, edited by Ippei Yamazawa. New York: Routledge, 2000.

Bergsten, C. Fred. *Whither APEC? The Progress to Date and Agenda for the Future.* Washington, DC : Institute for International Economics, 1997.

Morrison, Charles E. "Developing Cooperation in the 21st Century: Implications for APEC". *Asian Perspective* 21, no. 2 (1997): 37–56.

Zhang, Yunling. "China and APEC". In *Asia Pacific Crossroads: Regime Creation and the Future of APEC*, edited by Vinod K. Aggarwal and Charles E. Morrison. New York: St. Martin's Press, 1998.

GLOSSARY

ABAC	APEC Business Advisory Council
ABARE	Australian Bureau of Agricultural and Resource Economies
ABTC	APEC Business Travel Card
ADB	Asian Development Bank
AFS	APEC Food System
AFTA	ASEAN Free Trade Area
AIFN	APEC Infrastructure Facilitation Network
AMF	Asian Monetary Fund
APEC	Asia-Pacific Economic Cooperation
APERC	Asia-Pacific Research Centre
APIAN	APEC International Assessment Network
ASC	APEC Study Centre
ASTWeb	APEC Science and Technology Web
ATC EG	Agricultural Technical Cooperation Experts' Group
ATTT	Agriculture Technology Transfer and Training
BMN	Business Management Network
BOOT	build-own-operate-transfer
BVP	Business Volunteer Programme
CAPs	Collective Action Plans
CBN	Capacity Building Network
CGE	computable general equilibrium
CGP	Centre for Global Partnership
CTASC	Chinese Taipei APEC Study Centre
CTI	Committee on Trade and Investment
EBN	Energy Business Network
EC	European Community

Ecotech	Economic and Technical Cooperation
EDFOR	Education Forum
EDNET	Education Network
EGMEED	Expert Group on Minerals and Energy Exploration and Development
EPG	Eminent Persons Group
ESC	Ecotech Subcommittee
EVSL	Early Voluntary Sectoral Liberalization
EWG	(APEC) Energy Working Group
FAO	Food and Agriculture Organization
FDI	foreign direct investment
FEEEP	food, energy, environment, economic growth and population
GATS	General Agreement on Trade in Services
GCP	Good Clinical Practice
GDP	gross domestic product
GOS	Group on Services
HRD	human resource development
HRDWG	Human Resource Development Working Group
HURDIT	Human Resource Development Industrial Technology
IAP	Individual Action Plan
IEG	Investment Expert Group
IEGBM	Informal Experts Group on Business Mobility
IFAT	Implementation Facilitation Assistance Team
IGCC	Institute on Global Conflict and Cooperation
ILO	International Labour Organization
IMBN	International Molecular Biology Network
IMF	International Monetary Fund
IQAS	International Quality Assurance Systems
IST	Industrial Science and Technology
ISTWG	Industrial Science and Technology Working Group
IT	information technology
IWS	Infrastructure Workshop
JAPET	Japan-APEC Partnership for Education and Training
KFTC	Korean Fair Trade Commission
LMI	Labour Market Information (Group)
LSP	Labour and Social Protection (Network)
MAPA	Manila Action Plan for APEC
MFN	most-favoured-nation
MRA	mutual recognition agreement
MRC WG	Marine Resources Conservation Working Group
NAFTA	North American Free Trade Agreement
NBIP	Non-Binding Investment Principles

NEDM	Network on Economic Development Management
NGOs	non-governmental organizations
NPLs	non-performing loans
NTBs	non-tariff barriers
OAA	Osaka Action Agenda
OECD	Organization for Economic Cooperation and Development
PAFTAD	Pacific Trade and Development Conference
PECC	Pacific Economic Cooperation Council
RGCs	regional growth centres
RISE	Regional Integration for Sustainable Economies
SAT	science and technology
SCSC	Standards and Conformance Subcommittee
SIAPs	Summary of Individual Action Plans
SMEs	small and medium enterprises
SOM	Senior Officials Meeting
SSCs	Summary of Specific Changes
TIER	Taiwan Institute of Economic Research
TILF	Trade and Investment Liberalization and Facilitation
TRIMs	trade-related investment measures
UMAP	University Mobility in Asia and the Pacific
UNCTAD	United Nations Conference on Trade and Development
WTO	World Trade Organization

INDEX

B

C

E